DISCOVER
TABLE DECORATION

DISCOVER
TABLE DECORATION

40 ORIGINAL PROJECTS TO BUILD YOUR TABLE ARRANGING SKILLS

CHRISTOPHER HAMMOND

HAMLYN

First published in Great Britain in 1995 by Hamlyn,
an imprint of Reed Consumer Books Limited,
Michelin House, 81 Fulham Road, London SW3 6RB
and Auckland, Melbourne, Singapore and Toronto

SERIES PROJECT MANAGER: **MARY LAMBERT**
SERIES PROJECT ART MANAGER: **PRUE BUCKNALL**
ART EDITOR: **ALISON SHACKLETON**
STYLIST: **CAMILLA BAMBROUGH**
EXECUTIVE EDITOR: **JUDITH MORE**
ART DIRECTOR: **JACQUI SMALL**

PHOTOGRAPHS BY: **LUCY MASON**

ISBN: 0 600 58594 8

DTP ALISON SHACKLETON
ORIGINATION BY MANDARIN OFFSET, SINGAPORE
PRODUCED BY MANDARIN OFFSET
PRINTED & BOUND IN HONG KONG

CONTENTS

INTRODUCTION

Entertaining at home can be a very rewarding experience but can sometimes seem a little daunting, especially if you are catering for large numbers. Learning the art of table decoration through the projects in this book can help you overcome these worries and enable you to lay the table correctly for formal or informal dinner parties, do impressive napkin folds, make gifts for your party guests and create different floral decorations for the table's centrepiece.

Different forms of home entertaining, both in the home and in the garden, are covered in the book and range from large dinner parties to children's birthday parties and small intimate meals. Two projects have been included on more formal functions that are held at outside venues, such as weddings. Although some of the floral arrangements in the wedding section are for the more ambitious, there are other projects, such as almond bags, that are simple to make. Innovative ideas are also featured to help you entertain in style at festivals including Christmas.

The basic rules of table presentation are discussed in the Materials and Techniques section and it is here that you can pick up all the useful tips on what containers and other accessories you need to make a successful flower arrangement.

As time is always at a premium, many of the non-flower projects can be made in advance and stored away until needed, giving you more time free for food preparation on the day. Most of the floral arrangements can be changed to suit your requirements. With a little imagination they can be scaled down to any size to fit your table. They can also be changed to add in other materials that will emphasize the theme of your party .

Flowers are seasonal, although some of the varieties are now available throughout the year, so you will need to adapt some of the projects if they feature flowers only available in the summer, for example, and your party is due to be held during the winter months.

When you first attempt a project with flowers it is important to remember to buy them at their best for your party rather than to last as long as possible. Sometimes this may involve buying flowers a few days beforehand to let them open, or ordering them from your florist in advance to make sure that they will be at their peak on the day. Some flowers will also take longer to open and others may live only for a short time, so discuss the types of flowers you'd like to buy with your florist and buy them accordingly. Otherwise, you may find it difficult to make an attractive arrangement from a bunch of tightly closed lilies or rose buds. You will also need to organize the flowers well ahead of your proposed party, don't leave it until the day and to chance. Most florists and some stall holders will be happy to order certain flowers for a special occasion if you give them enough notice. The flowers might not always be available, so always think of a second choice.

During the spring months paper whites and daffodils with their fragrant scents and the ever-popular tulips can be included in your table displays. In summer delphiniums, larkspur, scabious, cornflower and nigella will provide an abundance of blues for your arrangements. In autumn when fewer flowers are available you can experiment with turning leaves, euphorbia and amaranthus to brighten up your table. In winter there is all the Christmas foliage to explore. Holly, spruce, pine cones and twigs can all be used in eye-catching displays. You can also include flowers that are available all year, such as spray daisy chrysanthemums, lilies and different varieties of roses.

Table decoration should be enjoyable and I hope the projects in this book inspire you to create some table settings that will be greatly admired by family and friends.

MATERIALS AND TECHNIQUES

Good food, a well-balanced menu, close friends and witty conversation are of course important elements to consider when organizing a dinner party, but all too often an attractive table presentation is forgotten about. A little time spent on creating the right atmosphere and some thought on a specific theme, colour and design can turn an ordinary dinner party into a special occasion.

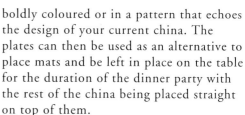

TABLE PRESENTATION

Starting right at the basics, the table you are using may be made from a beautiful dark wood that is polished to perfection. So you'll need to decide if you are going to display the table or cover it with a tablecloth to protect it. Nothing can beat a traditional white damask tablecloth, but you may prefer to use a coloured cloth to match the decor of your dining room or as a complete contrast. You could even make your own cloth out of a favourite fabric or one that matches your furnishings.

You probably already have a special dinner service that you use for parties and perhaps a second set of china that is for everyday use. You can always liven up the look of your service a little by using some underplates. Choose a larger plate than the dinner plate you already have that is

boldly coloured or in a pattern that echoes the design of your current china. The plates can then be used as an alternative to place mats and be left in place on the table for the duration of the dinner party with the rest of the china being placed straight on top of them.

Cutlery should always be spotlessly clean and well polished, especially if you are using a set that is silver. Generally, cutlery is arranged at either side of the plate, placed in the order that corresponds with the courses.

A FORMAL TABLE SETTING

If you were organizing a formal dinner party for important guests and serving a five-course meal a typical table setting would work in the following way. From the right-hand side working in toward the plate you would need: a bread or hors d'oeuvre knife, a soup spoon and a fish knife, a knife for the main course and nearest the plate the dessert spoon. From the left-hand side moving in toward the plate you would need: a hors d'oeuvre fork, a fish fork, a larger fork for the main course and lastly a dessert fork. If other cutlery is needed for extra, small courses it may be produced when the course arrives. Wine glasses work in the opposite way from the cutlery and should be used in

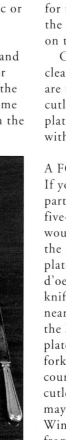

order from the plate outward, starting with a sherry glass, white wine glass, a larger glass for red wine and last of all a champagne flute (optional) to accompany the pudding. A water glass can also be placed behind the other glasses.

A crisp, freshly laundered napkin can be folded in many different styles to great effect. There are two examples, A Fan and A Jabot Napkin (*see pp. 18–19*) detailed in the project pages under the Entertaining in style section. The folded napkins can be placed on the main plate, on the side plate above the place setting, or arranged in a wine glass depending on how formal or informal you wish to be. When folding napkins into intricate designs you will find that using a spray-on starch will help them keep their shape.

Where to seat your guests is most important and if you are having a formal dinner party you will need to work this out in advance. The formal etiquette is for the host and hostess to sit at opposite ends of the table with the host at the head. On his right should sit the main female guest. The main male guest should sit to the right of the hostess. The order should then run male, then female all around the table. Couples should not be seated next to each other but be placed diagonally opposite each other. The dinner party food should always be served from the left and taken from the right of the guest.

AN INFORMAL TABLE SETTING

On most occasions you will find there is not enough room on your table for a formal dinner setting, so for normal entertaining at home an informal table setting would be used. This will automatically create a more comfortable atmosphere and immediately put all your guests at their ease.

To accommodate the lack of space, a more compact arrangement of cutlery is normally used. The butter knife can sit across the side plate, which is placed on the left. The starter cutlery or soup spoon can arrive with its course, or the starter can be pre-placed at each setting with the cutlery on its plate. The choice of cutlery will depend on the choice of menu, but

still the same golden rule will apply. Always start from the outside to the inside nearest the plate. Knives should be positioned on the right and forks on the left. Pudding spoons and forks can be placed nose to tail at the top of the plate, or they can just be brought in with the pudding itself.

Again, wine glasses should be used from the inside to the outside, but it is normal to use fewer glasses. A glass for wine and another for water is often sufficient. Seating should be more relaxed for an informal dinner party and will sometimes depend on the most convenient route to the kitchen for the host and hostess. It is quite acceptable to serve the food clockwise around the table.

After dinner coffee can be served at the table using coffee cups, and the glasses can be brought in for liqueurs or brandies when the coffee is served.

Once you have decided on the basic layout for your dinner party you can embellish the arrangement as much as you like. In the following chapters of this book you will find many different ways to set off a special meal and learn some of those extra special little touches to set off your table layout. You can even adapt some of the ideas to suit the different dining occasions that occur. Alternatively, you can use some of the projects as the starting point for your own imaginative ideas.

TIP

● Remember that many guests will have come by car and will appreciate a water glass for chilled mineral water or to use as an alternative to alcohol.

MATERIALS

At the start of each project there is a list of materials used, including such items as fabric, card, plastics and paints or flowers and foliage. The flower names given will generally be the ones most commonly used by florists. The varieties listed are just a guideline and can be substituted if they are unavailable or changed for a different colour scheme. The amount of flowers used is detailed in the projects but will need to be adjusted if you use a larger or smaller container, or if you create a different sized display.

Here is a collection of some of the equipment you will need for the projects contained in the book.

GENERAL EQUIPMENT
• Florist's foam
• Chicken wire containers
• Ribbons
• Paper rolls or plastic knives
• Cutting board
• Paints
• Wreath frames
• Ruler
• Pens
• Brushes
• Glue and hot glue gun
• Florist's wire
• Reel wire/stub wires
• Dried roses
• Stencils
• Plastic bags or sheeting`
• Floral fix

BUYING AND CONDITIONING FLOWERS

Once you have organized your table and selected the dinner service you will use for your party, select a colour or style theme and work out how you can best express this with your flowers.

When you buy your flowers they may have come straight from the market and have not been properly conditioned. They may also have been out of water for some time on your journey home from the florists, so they will need your special attention when you get them home. All flower stems seal gradually once they are out of water, even for ten minutes.

To condition bought flowers properly you should give them a good drink in a deep container, such as a bucket, for at least a day, before you start to arrange them. Cut off about an inch from their stems at an angle so they have a maximum surface area from which to absorb water. Do not bash the stems unless you find them impossible to cut. They will drink far better through a neat, clean cut than through a bruised stem.

Next you'll need to strip off all the foliage (and thorns if they have any) from below the water line. This will help keep the water clean and stop it from smelling. Place the flowers in freshly drawn water. Do not strip off too many of the leaves from your flowers by going too high up the stem. Remember you will need the foliage on stems for your arrangement. A good proprietary flower food that is dissolved in the water can help to make the flowers last longer.

When conditioning very long stems you may find it difficult to find a vase or bucket tall enough to support them. Try using chicken wire as an extension to the sides of your container to give it more height. You can always re-use the chicken wire for other projects.

If you are using lilies for your arrangement they may take a few days for the flowers to open. As soon as they show signs of opening and you can see the pollen on the anthers on the stamen, carefully pull each one out of the flower, leaving the central green one. If you leave

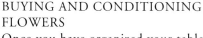

CANDLES

Throughout this book you will find many of the projects incorporate candles in their design. To avoid any accidents, make sure that the candles are always firmly secured in the floral arrangement and that their flames are well away from any flowers or foliage that might catch alight. Never leave lit candles unattended or in the presence of young children.

them in you will find they soon fluff out and drop pollen onto the petals and stain the flower. Also if the pollen brushes against curtaining, wallcoverings or clothing it will leave a deep orange mark that is difficult to remove. Each flower on the stem will open at a different stage so it is important to monitor their progress.

If you are using roses and find that they have not opened sufficiently on the day of your party, gently cradle the heads in your hand one at a time and blow into the petals to open them. But be careful not to blow too hard and damage the flowers.

CONTAINERS

You can use many types of container (see right) for your flower arrangements. Some can be prepared with chicken wire and florist's foam, some with just water. Containers, such as yoghurt or plastic pots, can also be easily slotted into more attractive baskets or other containers that are not watertight, such as the flowerpot on pages 30–31 (or right). If you use an inner container with a basket, choose some moss to wedge it firmly into place. For extra security you can always wire through the top of the inner container and attach it through the basket weave. Sometimes you may want to liven up a vase for a special occasion. By binding fabric around a suitable vase you can create a new and exciting container.

FLORIST'S FOAM

This absorbent foam is perfect to use for flower arranging as it holds the flowers' stems in place, enabling you to create the sort of arrangement you want. It is available in three different types from most good flower shops, wholesalers and some large supermarkets. "Wet" florist's foam is the type to use with fresh flowers, "Springtime" is suitable for flowers with soft stems, and "Dry" is the foam to use with dried flower arrangements.

Conical and sphere florist's foam shapes for containers such as candlesticks are also available in Wet and Dry foams. You can also obtain designer boards of Wet florist's foam from specialist stockists that can be cut to form specific shapes.

USING "WET" FLORIST'S FOAM

MATERIALS
Wet florist's foam
Container
Plastic sheeting
Sharp knife, reel wire

1

2

1 Fill a large container with water, ideally use a kitchen sink. Make sure that the water is deep enough and that the container is wide enough to move the block of florist's foam once it is soaked. If it touches the bottom of the container before it is soaked a tide line will appear and the area above will not absorb any water, making the florist's foam useless. If you have to wedge the foam into the container it will not soak properly. Also let the water settle before inserting the foam or it might get wedged in the container and not soak correctly. Once the water is still, place the florist's foam block on top of the water, then let go. The foam block should now be sinking until it is full of water and it reaches the container's bottom.

2 Once the block is soaked (see picture), take it out and refill the container with more water if

you need to soak other blocks. If your soaked block is not for immediate use, store it in water in another container. You can store one block on top of the other in a container topped up with water, but handle soaked blocks gently as in this state they are fragile and can easily break.

3 Place the soaked foam block on some plastic sheeting. Water will run out of it for a while and some will be squeezed out of it when you handle it. Cut it with a sharp knife or reel wire to fit into a small container.

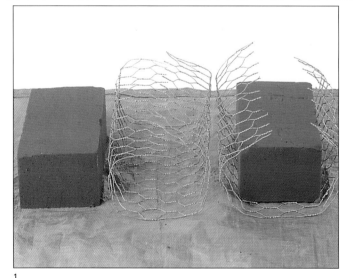

3

CHICKEN WIRE WRAPS

MATERIALS
Plastic sheeting
Soaked Wet florist's foam
16in (41cm) of Chicken wire, cut from roll (from DIY stores)
Cutters/scissors
Florist's plastic oblong tray
Florist's tape
Florist's plastic round container
Reel wire

1 Prepare the work surface with plastic sheeting. Take the florist's foam and the length of

chicken wire. Before you start to wrap the chicken wire around the block pre-bend it to the size of its four sides. This will create the shape needed without the wire cutting into the block's corners. Put the foam into the chicken wire shape and fold around the block.

2 Once wrapped, secure the block by bending the wire ends back on themselves with cutters or scissors.

3 Now fold back the ends of the chicken wire neatly as if wrapping a parcel. Take a plastic tray and push the block into position. Wedge it firmly between the sides of the container. Take some strong florist's tape and thread it through the side of one of the chicken wire loops.

4 Fold the sticky tape back onto itself, securing it onto the wire. Now pass the tape under the plastic tray to the other side sticking it as you go. Turn the block around and secure the tape onto the wire as before. Repeat at the other end to fix the block. It is now ready to use in arrangements such as the Wedding Top Table Flowers (see pp. 62–63).

5 To secure more than one block together stand the florist's foam blocks on their ends. Make a pre-folded shape out of a large piece of chicken wire and wrap it around all the blocks.

6 Twist up ends of the cut wire as Step 2, and fold over the chicken wire at the top like a parcel. Take a round container and puncture small holes in the side near the top with scissors to match the large block corners.

7 Place the wrapped florist's foam blocks in the container and attach some reel wire to the chicken wire nearest the corner of the blocks. To do this take a wire length and fold it in half for added strength. Take the bent end and thread it behind the chicken wire to about halfway, then twist ends together securing them on the wire strut. Now thread bent end through the container's hole and tighten. Take the loose wire end and twist with the bent end, fixing it onto the plastic container's edge. Wind some of the excess wire around the support, then trim. Repeat with the other corners until it is secured.

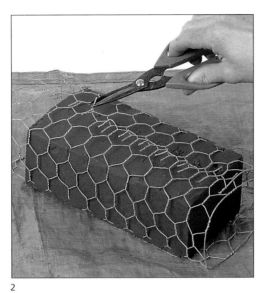

2

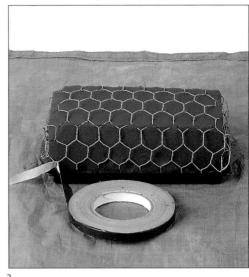

3

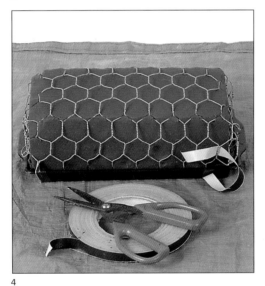

4

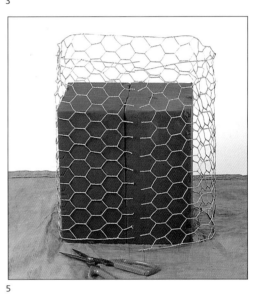

5

6

7

WIRING FLOWERS AND PAPPETS

MATERIALS
Stub wires
1 rose
Ribbon
Pine cones, walnuts, etc
Pappets

1 Flowers can be used without containers when wired in place, such as in the swagging for the buffet on pages 46–47. To attach flowers, take a stem of the chosen flower for your display and cut to the required length. Next take a wire to attach the stem onto the foliage of the project. You will have to judge what wire thickness to use to hold the flower in place. Now twist wire around the flower's stem, leaving enough wire to attach it to the foliage. Obviously, fresh flowers that are used in this way would have to be arranged at the very last moment and then kept fresh with a water mister or spray.

2 In the same way you can wire decorations, ribbons and pine cones or nuts onto arrangements. When wiring pine cones wrap a long stub wire around the gap in between the lower tiers of the seeds, bringing the ends of the wire together and twisting to secure. Once again, leave enough wire to fix the pine cone into place.

3 If a floral project is required to stay fresh for a longer time, such as the Hanging Wreath (see pp. 92–93) or the Valentine's Rose Candle Holder (see pp. 72–73), then pappets are the best way to keep the flowers looking good. These are small plastic vials with rubber tops that have a large enough hole to hold the flower's stem, but which are also tight enough to hold in all the water.

1

2

3

TIPS

● Always use the thinnest wire possible to wire flowers into place.

● Pappets can be cleverly concealed in a floral arrangement by placing them in the foliage and then adding a little moss on top.

● A few sizes of pappets are available so check the size of your flowers and their stem widths carefully before buying.

1

2

3

4

TIPS

● Another way of securing a bow in place is to wrap a stub wire around the horizontal line of the bow. You can use the long lengths of the wire to secure the bow firmly into the finished arrangement.

● You can attach a bow to a display by first pre-tying some ribbon around an object and using the free ends to fix it in the correct position.

5

MAKING A BOW

MATERIALS
Ribbon

Container

1 To make a bow to add to an arrangement, take a length of ribbon in one hand. Your free hand should be the most dominant one. Hold the ribbon with its shiny side toward you between your thumb and first finger. Leave a tail of ribbon that is a little longer than the desired loops of the bow hanging down. Take the ribbon above your thumb and first finger and twist it so that the dull side is turned around to face you.

2 Loop the ribbon around the back into the grip of your thumb and first finger. Make sure that the shiny side of the ribbon comes back over to face you. Gather the ribbon together and twist again so that the new tail has its dull side toward you.

3 Now bring the new tail in a loop up to meet your thumb and first finger. Bring the shiny side of the ribbon around to face you again and, as you are doing this, make a loop that is the same size as the first loop.

4 Imagine a horizontal line crossing between the loops at the point of your finger and thumb. Every even number should stay below this line and every odd number above it. Carry on making loops until the bow is just the size you wish it to be.

5 Now cut off the last tail, a little longer than the loops. Tie a length of ribbon along the imaginary horizontal line. Now use this length of ribbon to secure the tied bow firmly into place.

ENTERTAINING IN STYLE

A FORMAL DINNER PARTY

From time to time occasions arise that demand a more formal approach to entertaining, such as when business clients or important work colleagues are coming to dinner. For these meals it is important to observe the correct etiquette to create the right impression.

Once your table has been properly laid following the basic rules in Materials and Techniques on pages 8–9, you can embellish the arrangement as much as you wish. Preparation is important and so is timing, but all the projects for this party can be done well in advance. Flowers can be arranged earlier in the day and kept somewhere cool. The small gift boxes can be made in advance and if you've got children, they can help to make and decorate them. Fill the boxes with some hand-made chocolates to be consumed at the end of the meal, or maybe fill them with potpourri or a gift to make an elegant memento of your party.

EASY LEVEL

FORMAL NAPKIN FOLDS

Napkins can easily be prepared in advance. First launder, starch and press so that they can be folded into elaborate designs and stored until needed.

The two napkin folds shown here look complicated but are simple to make. Spray-on starch helps the napkins keep their shape, but ensure when ironing them that you keep the iron's surface clean from the spray starch.

For this table arrangement two napkin folds have been included. The more feminine fan fold (top right) can be used at each female's place setting at the table, and the more masculine jabot fold (right) can be positioned at each of the male's place settings.

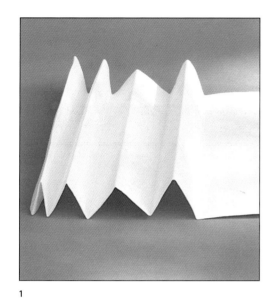

1

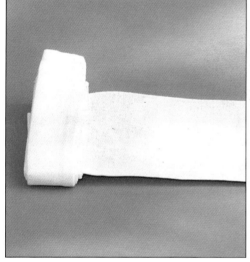

2

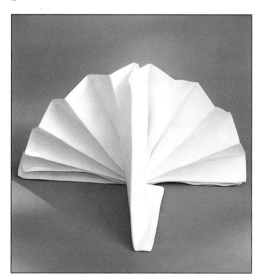

3

MATERIALS

Napkin

Spray-on starch

Iron

FAN NAPKIN (left)

1 First take a clean starched napkin and fold it in half lengthways. Pleat one end of the napkin evenly from the left side into the middle until just past halfway.

2 Bring the pleats together firmly and fold napkin in half again lengthways. Keep the pleats' edges together with one hand and fold the loose section of the napkin along the diagonal as shown here to make an angled shape for the support.

3 Tuck the overlapping section of the napkin underneath the balancing support you've made, then let the pleats of the fan fall open. Arrange the napkin on the table with the tail facing away from the guest.

JABOT NAPKIN (right)

1 Take a starched napkin, fold in half and half again to form a square. Keep the loose corners at the top right of the napkin. Fold the first layer down so the corners meet at the bottom left of the napkin to form a diagonal line from the top left to the bottom right of the napkin.

2 Bring the first layer back on itself to form a parallel fold to the diagonal fold, then repeat folding the corner back and forth until pleats form a zig-zag along the parallel strip. Repeat with second layer.

3 Fold a diagonal line from the bottom left corner to the top right by tucking the bottom right section under the top left half to form a triangle. Now tuck the two corner points into one another. Place napkin upright on table with the corners facing away from the guest.

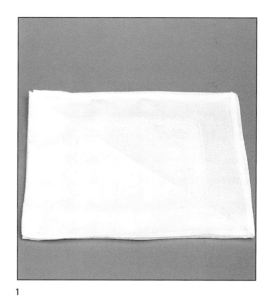

1

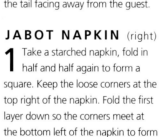

2

3

19

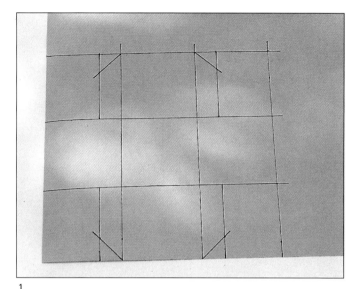

1

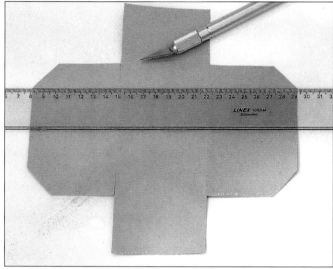

2

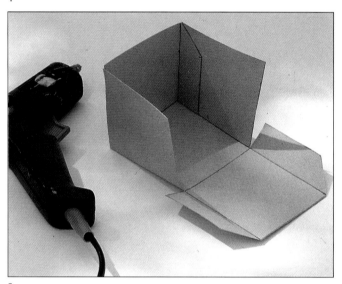

3

4

MATERIALS
(to make one box)
Marker pen or pencil
Strong pink card
Strong ruler
Scissors
Cutting mat
Paper craft knife
Strong glue/hot glue gun
Dried flowers such as Gerdo roses
Silver dusting powder
Chocolates, potpourri or a gift

1 Decide on the size that you want your gift box to be, then multiply this measurement by three. Draw a square with the ruler and marker pen onto the back of the chosen card making the sides equal to this second measurement. Divide the square you have drawn into nine equal squares. The measurement of these will be the same as your first, and will be the finished size of your box. Now carefully mark out four equal tabs and also draw in some cutting guides. Place two tabs on either side of the top central square and also do the same on either side of the bottom central square.

2 Cut out around the central cross shape incorporating the four tab shapes as shown here. Now place the card on a cutting mat and with a sharp craft knife and ruler score on the face of the card along the edges of the tabs and also the fold lines of the squares.

3 Carefully fold the box into shape and glue the tabs inside using a strong glue or a hot glue gun to keep it in position.

4 Make a box lid using a similar method to that of the box. Draw your central square about ⅛in

(3mm) larger than the square used for the box. To make the box lip draw a border about one-third of the width of your square around it. To make your tabs, extend every line of the central box out to the border edge, forming four small squares in the border's corners. Cut one line on each corner square and fold back the other line. Score and fold into shape as before and glue tabs into place under the lip to create your lid. Decorate by gluing on the dried flowers with strong glue or a hot glue gun and sprinkle silver dusting powder over the box. Add chocolates, potpourri or a gift as desired.

GIFT BOXES

These sophisticated gift boxes provide an attractive decoration for your dinner table and can hold delicious chocolates, sweet-smelling potpourri or a small token for your guests to take home. They can be made quite simply following the instructions provided. You can make them to any size, using materials that blend with your colour scheme. A strong card with an interesting texture has been used for these boxes, but you could use an alternative such as thick handmade paper or a heavy wallpaper.

The delicate, dusty pink colour of the card picks out the paler hues of the flower arrangement and especially the shade of the pink achillea, while the more masculine burgundy colour used for the poppy head boxes (*see main picture on pages 16–17*) links with the centre of the Stargazer lily.

Once the boxes are made they can be simply decorated with ribbon, or as shown here with dried flowers glued into position on the box lid. A silver dusting powder has been brushed onto the box to add an interesting finish.

AN EPERGNE ARRANGEMENT

A colourful and stylish flower arrangement provides the ideal focal point to your dinner table and also adds a personal touch to the occasion. You needn't spend a lot of time on the display but try adding in some soft foliage, country flowers and blackberries on the stem with the more cultivated flowers, such as Stargazer lilies, to create a less formal look.

Containers are also important and you can be as inventive as you like. If you do not own a formal epergne you can use many substitutes – attractive glass and ceramic containers can also work well. First of all choose a container that is the right size for your table. The one used for this project had to fill the centre of a long, wide table, so it needed to be quite large. It is an old nickel silver soup tureen bought from a junk shop, so it is not always necessary to bring out a treasured family heirloom.

If you find you are not going to use all your matching serving dishes for your meal, then you could use one, if it is large enough, for the floral display and to add a sense of continuity to your table theme.

1 Choose the container you are going to use for your arrangement and prepare it with the florist's foam that has been cut to size and wedged into the container or its liner. First insert the leatherleaf into the foam so that you start to form a rough outline of the shape you wish your arrangement to be. Now use the eucalyptus to form the length of your shape. Insert it from the side and trail it down to the table surface. Arrange more eucalyptus around the rest of the shape, leaving the stems a little longer than the leatherleaf. Then start to fill in with ivy trails, allowing them to follow the lines of the eucalyptus. And then add to the texture and appearance of the foliage with some stems of the attractive pink spot.

2 Follow the flowing lines of the eucalyptus with some stems of euphorbia at the two trailing ends of the arrangement, and then build up its shape by arranging stems of euphorbia around the sides, and also right at the top to give it some extra height. Now bring some colour into the foliage by inserting some antirrhinums, using two of them to mark the length of the arrangement, and place three more to form a triangular formation right along the top section.

3 Continue to place the antirrhinums around the circumference of your arrangement, putting three of the flowers on one side and two on the other. Fill out more of the circumference with the cream lisianthus, allowing the elegant lines of the flowers to cascade right down to the table surface. Spread these flowers throughout the body of the arrangement. Now add in all of the Stargazer lilies, placing them randomly among the other flowers in the display so that they give maximum effect.

1

2

3

4

5

6

MATERIALS
Container/liner
Soaked Wet florist's foam (see p. 12)
Scissors
1 bunch of leatherleaf
1 bunch of eucalyptus
1 bunch of ivy trails
1 bunch of pink spot (Hypoestes sanguinolenta)
10 stems of euphorbia
10 stems of antirrhinums
10 stems of lisianthus
7 stems of Stargazer lilies
10 stems of phlox
10 stems of achillea
10 stems of clover
Some stems of blackberries

4 Now that the arrangement is gaining height and has some definition, fill it out further with some stems of phlox that have been cut to the right size.

5 Cut down some stems of the pink achillea and then position them deep into the arrangement's foliage to give it more background depth. Then strategically place the longer remaining stems among the other flowers.

6 Next put in position the country clover flowers to give some softness to the arrangement. Finish off the display by inserting the blackberry stems to add extra texture and interest. Remember to remove all the thorns before you use them, handling the stems carefully with some thick gloves.

AN INFORMAL LUNCH PARTY

The projects that have been chosen for this informal lunch or dinner party are designed to evoke a welcoming and relaxing atmosphere on a warm summer's day.

The collection of terracotta flowerpots strewn casually across the table instantly creates a Mediterranean feel to the room and will soon put any guests at ease. The large flowerpot used with an inner plastic container makes an unusual vase for fresh flowers and along with the smaller flower pots of herb plants and dried flowers they establish the theme of a summer garden brought into your dining room.

The stippled tablecloth with its subtle green hues provides a fresh backdrop to the handpainted crockery and gives a natural-looking contrast to the earthy terracotta flowerpots.

Choose your napkins in blending greens to match the tablecloth and glasses. You could also extend the use of the flowerpots by making some into candle holders using the same method to make them as for the first dried flowerpot (*see p. 28*).

| EASY LEVEL |

DRIED ROSE AND HERB POTS

These small flowerpots filled with herbs or dried flowers make unusual table decorations. Used together they can be scattered randomly among the place settings to give a rustic feel to the lunch. Try to choose herbs that complement your menu and that will add a delicate aroma to the food.

The pots can be given to guests at the end of the meal as a parting token, perhaps reserving the herb plants for all the aspiring cooks.

1

2

1 Prepare both flowerpots with dry florist's foam. To do this take a block of dry foam and upturn the flowerpot onto it. Press down to make an indentation of the pot's opening. Remove the pot and carve away the foam until you have a shape that will fit into the flowerpot. Wedge or glue the foam in place. Leave enough room for the moss to sit on top of the foam, then place it in position. For the second pot, cut the foam as before, but wedge the flat surface into the pot leaving the cone-shaped end to protrude, carving it to the required shape. Place moss around the rim of the flowerpot and cut the heads off some Gerdo roses, leaving a bit of stem to secure in the foam. Arrange in a row around the pot's edge .

2 Take the contrasting Jacaranda roses for the first flowerpot and cut to the required length, leaving enough stem to secure them into the foam. Arrange in a regimented fashion lining up the heads one by one, pushing them into the pot through the moss until they form a square shape. For the second flowerpot add in more Gerdo roses until they cover the foam shape, filling in with moss as you proceed.

DRIED ROSE POTS

MATERIALS
2 small terracotta flowerpots
Dry florist's foam
Knife
Glue
Bun or carpet moss
Scissors
Dried Gerdo roses
Dried Jacaranda roses

1

2

HERB POTS

MATERIALS

Basil (dark opal) herb plant

Thyme (silver queen)
herb plant

2 small terracotta flowerpots

Polythene sheet or plastic bag

Potting compost, if required

Scissors

Bun, carpet or sphagnum moss

1 First take the basil and thyme herb plants, or others you have selected, and make sure they are well watered. Leave them to drain before repotting. Choose terracotta flowerpots that are the appropriate size for each plant and for the best result choose ones that have been well weathered. Line them with a strong polythene sheet or plastic bag, pushing it to the bottom of each flowerpot. Now gently shake out the herb plants from their plastic containers and transfer them into the terracotta pots. Push firmly into place, adding more potting compost if it is necessary. Next cut off all the excess plastic liner as close to the top of the flowerpot as is possible.

2 Now take some moss and cover the surface of the soil and use it to hide any of the liner that is still visible. If your pots don't look very weathered, it is possible to encourage mould to grow on the outside of them by brushing beaten egg lightly onto the terracotta and leaving it for some time outdoors. Alternatively, you could try to decorate them with some emulsion paint or attempt a stipple paint effect to echo the effect of the tablecloth project on pages 32–33.

MATERIALS

1 terracotta flowerpot
Plastic container
Soaked Wet florist's foam (*see p. 12*)
Scissors
Knife
Water
Bun moss
7 stems of rosemary
1 bunch of small-leafed eucalyptus
10 stems of astilbe
10 stems of nigella (love-in-the-mist)
10 stems of Osiana roses, thorns removed

INTERMEDIATE LEVEL

A FRESH FLOWER POT

Fresh flowers and interesting foliage arranged loosely in a jug or more unusual container can provide an eye-catching centrepiece that everyone will admire for an informal lunch party. They can also help to give a casual, relaxed feel to the gathering.

Look for different rustic containers to use or try adapting everyday utensils, such as this garden flowerpot.

Normally, it could never contain water as the terracotta material it is made from is porous and like most garden containers it has a water drainage hole in the bottom of the pot. But by slotting in a protective inner container it is transformed into a simple but effective vase that can hold fresh flowers. Use a wedge of florist's foam to anchor the flower stems at the container's base.

Suitable inner containers are very easy to find. Many products that you buy from supermarkets are packaged in watertight plastic containers. Once empty, these can be easily cut down and adapted to use as an inexpensive inner lining time and time again.

1

2

1 Once you've chosen a suitable terracotta flowerpot select a plastic container that will fit into it. Next you need to cut a small piece of the florist's foam and wedge it into the bottom of the plastic liner.

2 Fill the plastic container to about two-thirds full with water and place it into the terracotta flowerpot. Wedge it in place using some bun moss. Fill in the gap between the plastic container and the flowerpot with more bun moss until the level of moss reaches the top of the flower pot rim and disguises the plastic container completely. Before inserting the foliage and flowers, remove excess leaves from the bottom of the stems as this will help to keep the water fresher for longer.

3

4

3 To create the foliage outline of the shape you require arrange the rosemary in the small piece of foam, anchoring the stems in position. Add in some stems of eucalyptus for added contrast.

4 Fill out the foliage with more eucalyptus, building up into a stronger shape, then take some stems of astilbe and arrange them in the foam. Visually divide the arrangement into thirds and arrange one stem in each section.

5

6

5 Continue to insert more astilbe running throughout the entire arrangement. Now add some nigella or love-in-the-mist. Place the stems randomly in the pot to give a more natural, unstructured effect. The nigella used is one of the darkest varieties, but the flowers also range in colour from pale powder blues through to white.

6 Next take three Osiana roses and insert them in the middle of the arrangement. Dot the remainder around the circumference, placing a few at varying levels.

INTERMEDIATE LEVEL

A STIPPLED TABLECLOTH

When you're trying to create a special theme, such as for this informal lunch party, tablecloths can become an integral part of the finished effect. They can be chosen to blend with your decor and to enhance your dinner service and the other featured accessories.

Obviously, you can search for an appropriate tablecloth in the shops, but it can be much more fun to make your own. You can liven up an old plain or stained tablecloth or even use a white sheet. Here different shades of green fabric paint have been used to create a stipple paint effect. Fabric paints should be widely available from craft shops, but you can also obtain them by mail order from different companies (*see p. 112*). The paints come in many shades, so you can choose different colours if you want to change the colour scheme. Always use at least three shades to achieve the best effect, first starting with the strongest colour to create the necessary depth, then going on to highlight the cloth with the lighter colours.

1

2

3

4

1 Prepare the surface you will be working on with some plastic sheeting to allow for any paint spillage. A kitchen floor would be ideal to spread out on so you can get an overall view of the tablecloth. Start stippling with the darkest of all the green colours (or the darkest of the ones you have chosen). Mix the fabric paint on an old saucer or disposable foil plate. Load your paintbrush with just enough paint and wipe any excess onto a rag. Using a light touch, randomly stipple some splodges of paint with the brush over the tablecloth. Next blend in all the paint using a circular motion with the paintbrush. Keep repeating this painting action until you have covered the whole of the tablecloth with your first coat of fabric paint.

2 Next choose the paint shade that is closest to the first colour you have used. Work through all your greens from the darkest first, until you come to the lightest of your colours. Use this slightly lighter paint in the same way as you did the first, using the stippling method carefully over the paint already on the cloth until you have completely covered all of it with the second colour.

3 Now use the lighter shade you have chosen to highlight over the dark areas and to blend together the colours until you achieve a mottled effect over the entire tablecloth. Use some white paint on any areas that have become too dark to bring through the whiteness of the cloth, or if your cloth has a base colour to begin with, try to get a paint that matches it to go over the dark areas.

4 Let the paint dry overnight and then iron the tablecloth with a hot iron, following the fabric paint manufacturer's instructions, to seal the fabric paints. Iron all over the tablecloth until you are satisfied that you have sealed in all the paint. Now you can wash the tablecloth as directed on the fabric paints to bring back its texture and iron it once again. You may now wash the tablecloth as often as you wish safe in the knowledge that the green colours are firmly fixed on the material and will not run.

33

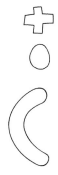

MATERIALS

Plastic tumblers, washed and free from grease

Coloured self-adhesive protective film, available from craft and design shops

Pen or pencil

Scissors

A CHILDREN'S PARTY

Organizing a themed children's party can be fun but forward planning is a must. The stencilled tablecloth and decorated tumblers can be made in the evenings of the weeks before the party. Assemble the gift bags in advance too, just slotting in the flowers at the last minute. After some work on the basket the party flowers are simple to make.

EASY LEVEL

PARTY TUMBLERS

Young children will love the clowns party theme that also appears on these glasses. Plastic tumblers are resilient and inexpensive to use and they are decorated with a big smiling face of a clown made from easy-to-stick film. They can be used during the party and then taken home as an extra present.

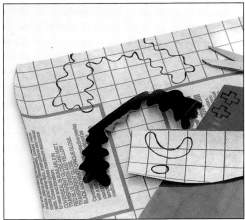

1

2

1 For this project, keep your design very simple or use the pattern provided on this page and enlarge it on a photocopier to the size you need. First take your plastic tumblers and decide how large your design should be. Draw it onto some stiff card, then cut it out into the various pieces to use as patterns to draw around. Choose the coloured film you wish to use for each shape and mark your patterns, reverse side up onto the back of the appropriate sheet. Alternatively, use tracing paper to transfer the design on this page in the same way onto your sheet of coloured film. The reverse method ensures that when you have cut out your shape it will be the correct way round. This is very important if your design involves letters or numbers.

2 Once you have cut out all the shapes that make up your clown design, peel off the film's backing paper as you put the shapes in position. Start with the hair shape, carefully fixing it in place. Align the straight edge with the rim of the glass and then ease the rest of the shape onto the plastic tumbler, smoothing out any air bubbles as you go. You have now got the outline of the face. Next fill in the clown's features working from the top down. Position the eyes, the nose and finally the mouth. Once the glasses have been completed and the adhesive is firmly fixed, the design will be permanent and the tumblers can then be hand washed normally. It is not advisable, however, to wash the glasses in a dishwasher.

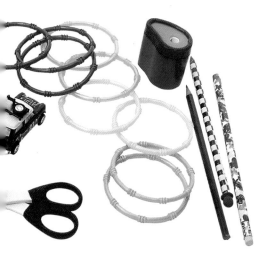

INTERMEDIATE LEVEL

PARTY BAGS

The gerberas in the fresh flower arrangement are also used here to make party bags. A simple daisy design inspired by children's drawings features on the bags, but contains a real flower with a special stalk and leaves. Young children will love this concept and will be rushing to take these novel bags home. They are not difficult to make and can be quickly assembled from strong card.

The coloured rope was obtained by the metre from a ship chandler's shop. When you cut it to size, just wrap some sticky tape around the cutting point to stop the ends fraying. Once you have cut through the tape take it off again and singe the cords' ends carefully over a flame to neaten them.

The gerberas can be slotted into place on the day and kept fresh with pappets (*see p. 14*).

The finished party bags can be filled with inexpensive gifts such as note pads, colouring books, crayons and some small toys. They make delightful presents for all the young partygoers at the end of a successful party.

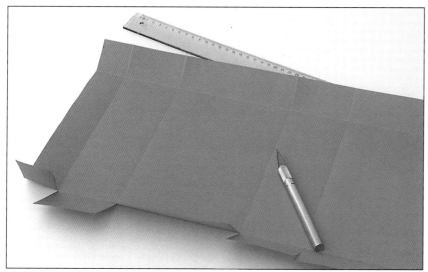

1

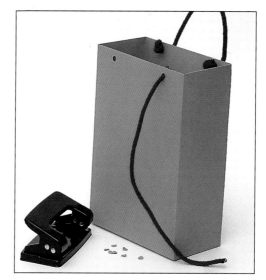

2

MATERIALS

(to make one bag)
1 sheet each of blue and green thick card
Pencil
Ruler
Sharp paper craft knife
Paper glue
Hole punch
Thick cord
Scissors
Gerbera
Sticky tape
A pappet filled with water
Gifts

3

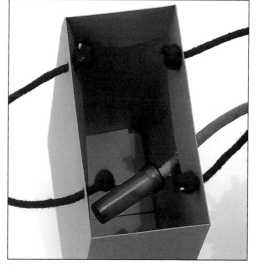

4

1 Take the blue card and mark out with the pencil and ruler the bag's rectangular size on the back – 18in x 12in (46cm x 30cm). Then draw vertical lines at intervals along the 18in (46cm) edge. The first line after 1½in (4cm), the second after 2¾in (7cm), the third after 5½in (14cm), the fourth after 2¾in (7cm), leaving a 5½in (14cm) gap between this line and the card edge. Now make two horizontal lines – the first line 1½in (4cm) from the top of the card and the second 2¼in (6cm) above the card's bottom edge. Score along these lines on the card's front with the craft knife. This will help to

form creases. Along the bottom section of the card cut along the vertical lines until you reach the horizontal line to form tabs. Fold in the top 1½in (4cm) to form a reinforced edge. Now fold the bag into shape from the left along the scored lines tucking in the 1½in (4cm) tab under the reinforced top edge. Glue into position. Next tuck in the bottom tabs, folding in the shorter ones first then the two largest. Glue these last two together for the base.

2 With a hole punch make two holes through the reinforced front section and two holes at the

back. Cut two lengths of cord for the bag's handles. With each cord tie a knot in one end and thread the other through one of the holes from the inside at the top of the bag. Pull through until the knot holds over the hole, then thread through the other hole from the outside and secure with a knot inside.

3 Cut out a stem from green card and glue it to the front of the bag. Next cut out two leaf shapes and glue them close to the stem's base. Form a hole with a craft knife just above the top of the stem to hold the flower. (If you are making

the bag in advance stop here and finish by inserting the fresh flower and pappet on the day of the children's party.)

4 Cut a gerbera stem to size and thread it through the hole and fix a pappet onto the stem's end. Pull the stem gently through until the gerbera is flush with the side of the bag. Attach the pappet inside with sticky tape. Fill the bag with all your chosen novelty gifts. Save the remaining green card to make more stems and leaves, then carry on making more of the party bags using the same method.

1

2

3

4

1 First take the basket you have chosen for the arrangement and spray it with red spray paint. Make sure that you get an even coverage by using two coats. Leave it to dry between coats, then take a plastic container that will easily fit into the basket and wedge in it some florist's foam. Place the prepared plastic container into the basket ensuring that the foam is proud of the rim of the basket. If the sides of the basket are too high for your inner container, raise the level of the inner container with tissue paper or moss until it is in the correct position. You will need as much foam as possible above the

edge of the basket so that you can arrange the flowers and foliage in a horizontal fashion into the foam block. Now wedge the inner container in place in the basket with moss. Build up the moss until it reaches the rim of the basket and hides the sides of the container.

2 Arrange the stems of leatherleaf in the foam to form the basic shape you want your arrangement to be. Next build up with some yellow mimosa, arranging it evenly throughout the basket. Keep the flowers' stems slightly longer than those of the leatherleaf.

3 Take all the coloured ribbons and hold them together around the middle. Take a thick stub wire and bend it around the ribbons. Pull it together and twist the legs of the wire until they hold the ribbons in place. Next, insert the wire legs into the foam positioning the ribbons around the basket. For extra safety, instead of a stub wire you can use a plastic strip cut from an old washing-up container. Tie it around the ribbons and then insert it in the foam.

4 Now arrange the large-headed gerberas in the basket, keeping the stems a little shorter than those

of the mimosa. Make a circle around the edge of the basket with the red and yellow gerbera flower heads, keeping the stems horizontal and the heads lifted slightly upward. Fill in the top section with more gerberas until the basket is full. Once the arrangement is finished and the coloured helium balloons have arrived, wire the long ribbons attached to them together with a stub wire and secure the wire's legs firmly into the basket's foam. Experiment with all the balloons until you can get them to float together at different heights (see the main picture detailed on page 34).

CHILDREN'S PARTY FLOWERS

The circus theme is echoed here in this floral display in the brightness of the coloured ribbons and the balloons, but mostly in the large-headed red and yellow gerbera flowers. They are very reminiscent of the over-sized flowers worn in clown's buttonholes.

You can liven up an old basket to coordinate with your colour scheme by spray-painting it in a bright primary colour. The red used here sets off the gerberas perfectly and the bright yellow mimosa has been arranged in the basket to give added fullness.

Helium balloons are loved by all children and it is worth spending that bit extra to have them delivered on the day, blown up and tied ready for wiring into the floral basket. Don't forget to order the right colours and to get enough for all the party guests.

MATERIALS
1 wicker basket
Red spray paint
Plastic container
Soaked Wet florist's foam (*see p. 12*)
Carpet moss
I bunch of leatherleaf
1 bunch of mimosa
Strips of coloured ribbon, cut into 10in (25cm) pieces
Stub wires
10 red and yellow gerberas
Several helium balloons

39

1 Take the two stencil sheets and draw your design onto the shiny side with the pen. On the first sheet draw the first shapes to paint. Mark with dots the second shapes to be painted. Mark out the second colours to paint on the second sheet, marking in dots the first colours. If you use the design on page 41, place the stencil over it (or increase its size by using a photocopier), shiny side up. Mark "one" in the corner and trace around the black lines and mark out the red shapes with dots. Mark your second sheet "two" and trace around the red lines and mark out the black lines with dots. On a cutting mat cut around all the solid lines leaving dotted lines of sheet one and do the same with sheet two.

2 Cover your work table with sheeting and spread out your tablecloth. Spray stencil sheet one lightly with adhesive on the dull side in a well-ventilated room. Press the stencil firmly down onto the cloth.

3 Paint in shapes with the stencil brush and paints using a circular motion (red, black and mauve paints have been used here). Don't use too much paint as it could run. When you've painted all the shapes, remove stencil and leave to dry.

4 Spray sheet two with adhesive and place on cloth. Align the dotted shapes over the coloured areas and press down firmly.

5 Fill in the next shapes with yellow and green and again use red. Remove stencil sheet and allow clown to dry overnight. If you are making a pattern, wash the stencil sheets with warm soapy water and dry, then repeat from step two.

6 Finally, seal the clowns by ironing following the paint manufacturer's instructions and wash cloth to remove adhesive.

1

2

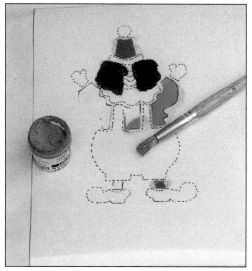

3

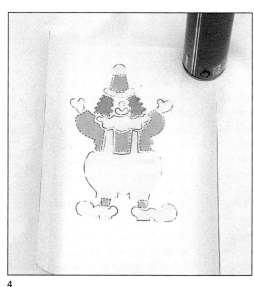

4

5

6

MATERIALS
2 A4 sheets of plastic stencil
Permanent ink marker pen
Craft knife
Cutting mat
Plastic sheeting
Tablecloth
Temporary spray adhesive
Stencil brush
Fabric paints
Iron

ADVANCED LEVEL

CLOWN CLOTH

The clown motif has again been used with this stencil design for a tablecloth. It helps to give emphasis to the theme and pulls together all the colours used for the party and the projects in this section. These jolly painted clowns bring the circus atmosphere right into this birthday celebration.

For this project you could use an old tablecloth that you do not often use, or the stencil effect could work just as well on a paper one. Another alternative is to use a new, plain single sheet. Once it has been decorated and the party has passed, it could be put into use on a child's bed. You could also do a matching pillowcase.

Using the clown stencil on this page, just trace out two clown designs onto the stencil sheets. Draw the outline on the shiny side with a permanent marker. Sheet one should follow the black-lined shapes for the first colours; sheet two should follow the red lines of the second set of colours to paint.

Fabric paints are readily available, but you can also get them by mail order (*see p. 112*).

41

MATERIALS

Clean and polished glass
containers

Mixed houseplants

Pulses such as lentils and
red kidney beans

Jug

1

2

1 Choose a glass container for its clean lines, straight sides and size. Ideally use a wide dish as pictured here.

2 Next group your houseplants with the taller ones placed together at the back of the container. Bring all the shorter plants to the front. (Water the plants well first and let any excess water completely drain away.)

3 Arrange the smaller trailing plants, such as ivies, close to the front edge of the container so that the leaves can trail attractively down the side. Next fill a jug with your chosen pulses and pour them into the dish right up to the top. Make sure that you use enough pulses so that the tops of the plant pots cannot be seen.

4 For an alternative tall glass vase design take your container and fill it from a jug of pulses, but remember to leave enough room to place your chosen houseplant.

5 Sit the houseplant firmly on the pulses and with the jug pour the remainder of the pulses into the container, covering the sides and the top of the plant pot completely.

3

4

5

EASY LEVEL

OUTDOOR HOUSEPLANTS

An evening drinks party held in the garden, or on a balcony, would be ideal for this project. The arrangement's design follows on from the idea of bringing the garden to your dining table used in the informal dinner party, but this time does the opposite. It introduces glass vases, containers and houseplants normally used inside to an outdoor setting.

A BUFFET MEAL

When catering for a large number of people a buffet-style reception can be the easiest solution, whether you are holding the party at home, in the garden, or at a hired venue.

The buffet meal enables guests at a large gathering to circulate freely and mingle. Whatever the occasion you're celebrating you will find that a buffet sets an informal atmosphere and soon gets your guests into a party mood.

By adorning the buffet table with attractive swagging and flower trees you immediately make it the main focal point of the party. Make sure the food is stylishly arranged so that it looks good and is accessible to your guests.

MATERIALS
(to make 1 swag)
2 stems of ruscus
Stub wire
Scissors
2 stems of trailing ivy
2 stems of box
Reel wire
Pins
Clothed table
1 bunch each of tansy, achillea, carthamus, cornflowers, scabious, border pinks and crocosmia
2 stems of lisianthus
2 stems of daisy chrysanthemums

INTERMEDIATE LEVEL

FLORAL SWAGGING

When you decorate the buffet table, think about its function and leave the most space to display the food. One area that will not be affected by this is the side of the table and swagging flowers and foliage around the table's circumference can be very effective. Remember to secure the swagging firmly onto the tablecloth as inevitably people will brush against the table when helping themselves to the food. To keep the flowers looking fresh, especially on a hot summer's day, spray them thoroughly with a water mister just before your guests arrive.

1 Take two stems of ruscus and wire together with a stub wire to form the first long swag. Twist the wire ends together firmly to form a secure extension.

2 Cut the ivy into sections and attach with stub wires to the ruscus, then similarly add in the box. Continue until you have a thick, even swag of foliage with some of the ivy trailing down a little.

3 Once your foliage swag is complete, bind around some reel wire for strength. Next present the swag against the tablecloth and secure it by taking a pin and piercing the cloth at the table's corner. Push the pin through again so the pin is attached to the tablecloth. Hold the swag in position and pass the point of the pin between the stems of the foliage. Now pass the pinpoint through the tablecloth again to hold swag in place. Repeat with other end.

4 Take the tansy and cut the stems down close to the flowerhead. Wrap a stub wire around the stem leaving two legs of wire (*see Wiring Flowers p. 14*). Now place the flower on the swag. Twist the wire legs around the foliage to hold it in position. Insert all the tansy heads in this way, scattering them all randomly.

5 Repeat this process with the achillea heads for an even spread of yellow through your swag. Now do the same with the orange carthamus, then build up more colour with the cornflower heads. Some lighter flowers can be held in place by threading their stems through the other existing stems.

6 Add in the scabious, border pinks, crocosmia and lisianthus flower heads until you have a rich-textured and colourful swag, then highlight with daisy chrysanthemums.

1

2

3

4

5

6

1

4

MATERIALS

Trunk or branch, cut to size
Saw, hammer and nails
Terracotta flowerpot
Scissors
Bin liner
Chicken wire
Quick-drying cement
Carpet moss
Soaked Wet florist's foam (*see p.12*)
2 bunches each of box and ruscus and one of ivy trails
1 bunch each of tansy, achillea, carthamus, cornflower, scabious, border pinks, crocosmia, chrysanthemums cut to heads, lisianthus

FLOWER TREES

There are two reasons why these flower trees are perfect for decorating a buffet. Firstly, their containers have narrow bases that take up little table space. Secondly, their height allows the arrangement to be above all the food on the table. Make sure that your tree (or trees) will not topple over by compensating for its height with a stable container filled with cement. Trunks for the trees can be found in the wild or bought from florists.

2

3

5

6

1 Take your tree's trunk. It does not matter if it is bent as it will add to the natural look. Hammer in two nails at each side just down from the top. Cover the drainage hole in the flowerpot with a bin liner and position the trunk in the pot. Wedge it in place with chicken wire until it stands unaided.

2 Mix up some quick-drying cement in a bucket and pour into the container. Make sure the cement is deep enough to hold the tree trunk in place. Leave overnight to set. Cover over the cement and chicken wire with moss. Next wrap about half a block of florist's foam in chicken wire. Cut a hole in the bottom to make room for the trunk. Wedge the foam block firmly onto the tree trunk until it reaches the nails. Leave enough room in the top of the foam for all the stems.

3 Arrange stems of box foliage, cut to size, in the foam and form a ragged ball. Place them so they radiate out from the centre.

4 Now take some ruscus and ivy trails and arrange in a similar way. Let these stems protrude from the circle made with the box.

5 Start to add in the tansy and achillea for an even yellow coverage. Again, the flowers should radiate from the centre of the foam from all angles. Insert some upside down, pushing their stems firmly into the foam. Next fill out the tree with carthamus, letting its foliage hide the foam. Next insert the softer stems of the cornflowers before the foam becomes massed with stronger stems, then build up the blue colour with the scabious.

6 Finish off by filling out the flower tree with the border pinks, crocosmia, chrysanthemum heads and lisianthus.

49

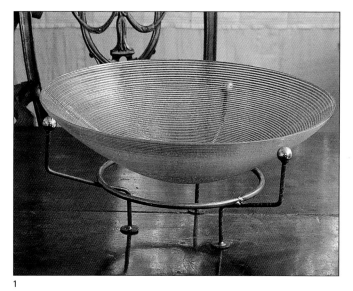

1

2

3

4

1 Choose a glass container that has a very wide opening but that is quite shallow. The one used here is perfect as it is made from strong thick glass and is supported by an elegant iron stand. Place your container in its chosen position on the table as it will be very difficult or awkward to move later on when it is full of water.

2 Fill your container to the required level with water from a jug. Leave room at the top to allow for any accidental movement of the table. If the table is nudged and the bowl is too full, the water could spill over and spoil your tablecloth. Food dye can be used at this point if you wish to colour the water, but this works best without adding any flowers as the orchids will take up the dye and and this will ruin their natural looks. (Keep a cloth handy to mop up any water that spills over onto the table.)

3 Cut the orchid heads from their stems with the scissors, leaving enough of the stem attached to the flower head to enable them to "drink" properly. Next place the orchids gently, one at a time, onto the surface of the water.

4 Once all the orchids are in position, drop the floating candles into the water by holding their wicks and lowering them gently onto the surface of the water. Make sure that all the wicks stay dry. Shortly before your guests start to arrive, light all the candles. But do not ever attempt to light the candles out of the water as you could easily burn your fingers trying to lower them into the water.

FLOATING CANDLES

Soft candlelight instantly creates an intimate atmosphere at any dinner table. By floating candles in a bowl you create an unusual centrepiece, whether it is used as a focal point for a table setting or is placed on a side table for a drinks party.

The water too gives out a relaxing quality and with the freedom of the floating objects you can achieve an ever-changing display. Take care not to overload the surface of the water, but keep the arrangement simple and minimal to echo the simple Japanese style of presentation. The exotic orchids that are widely used in the Orient help to enhance this theme.

Oriental culture has always respected the natural forces and eastern peoples believe it is good luck to have these forces represented at home. In this design the four elements are brought together in close harmony. The flowers that are grown in the soil represent "Earth". "Water" and "Fire" are evident in the water and lit candles, and the flames burning the air represent "Wind".

MATERIALS
Glass container
Water
Jug
Cloth
Phalaenopsis orchids
Scissors
Floating candles
Matches

51

SPECIAL OCCASIONS

A WEDDING

To arrange the flowers at a large wedding takes a great deal of planning, organization and experience, but you could get together with some friends and combine your talents.

For a smaller wedding you could just use a few of these ideas to create the reception flowers for a good friend or relative. You could choose one of the projects, such as the cake table decoration or the candlestick arrangement, and make it your own personal contribution.

Always consult closely with the bride-to-be and ask to see sketches of

her dress to get the feel of the wedding style. Get some fabric swatches from her, and take them with you when you buy the flowers. Settle on the colour scheme and the flowers to include, making sure that they will be available at the time of the wedding, as you will probably be planning well ahead. You may need another meeting nearer the day for any last minute changes.

Organize a time with the caterers or the restaurant when you will be able to deliver the flowers or arrange them on-site. Make sure your designs suit the venue – look at its decor, the size of the tables and the room's dimensions – before finalizing your ideas.

MATERIALS
(to make one almond bag)
1 average-sized dinner plate
White silk
Dressmaker's chalk
Dressmaking scissors
1 large dinner plate
Net
Silver and gold sugared almonds
White wired ribbon

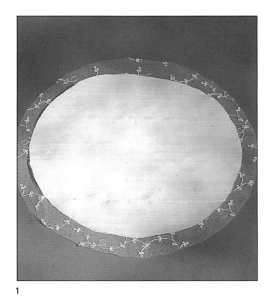

1

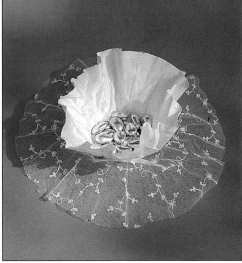

2

3

4

EASY LEVEL

ALMOND BAGS

These traditional bags that contain sugared almonds are stylish to look at and make attractive presents to decorate the wedding table at each female place setting. The best effect is achieved when they are made from the same fabric as the bride's or bridesmaids' dresses, and are finished with an attractive toning ribbon. Here we've used some white silk covered with net to make the bags.

The bags are very simple to make so do not worry if you have a lot of guests to make them for – once you get started you will soon finish them quickly. Plan how much material you need by using the method described in Step One and then try making the bags in batches of ten to stop your job becoming too repetitive. Prepare them well in advance of the wedding and make a few extra in case you find that the acceptance numbers have changed at the last moment.

Unless you are making the bags months ahead, you can fill them as you make them because the sugared almonds will keep for a long time.

1 To calculate how much silk material you'll need for the bags, lay the average-sized dinner plate on a sheet, measure it, and then multiply by the number of guests to find the amount of material needed. Do the same for the netting but use a large dinner plate. To make the bags, first spread out your white silk and place the average-sized dinner plate on top. Draw carefully around the plate template with the dressmaker's chalk and then remove it. Cut out the circle with a pair of dressmaking scissors. Now select a slightly larger plate to use on the netting and cut out the material in the same way. Place the two cutouts together, with the right side of the silk fabric facing downward on top of the net.

2 Place an appropriate amount of sugared almonds in the middle of the silk circle – about 20 almonds should be enough. Draw up the sides of the silk until they cover the almonds and gather the material together in your hand to form a neck to the bag.

3 Now do the same with the netting in a slightly looser fashion. Cut a length of ribbon and tie it around the neck you have just formed. The ribbon used here has wired edges that can be easily shaped into a beautiful bow.

4 Next cut a longer length of ribbon and form two loops on either side of its centre point. Now place this bow shape against the tie around the bag of almonds. Secure it in position using the legs of the tie to form a knot. Primp the bow into an attractive shape (see p. 15 for Making a bow).

1

2

3

4

MATERIALS

Clothed table/plastic sheeting
Wedding cake
Scissors
Ivy trails, large flat ivy leaves
Reel wire
Stub wire
5 Le Reve lilies, stems cut short
1 bunch of scabious, stems cut short
5 stems of Valerie roses, cut short
1 bunch of white nigella, stems cut short
5 stems of cow parsley, cut short
1 stem of light blue delphinium

1 Work on the cake table in situ. First cover the area around the table with plastic sheeting to contain your mess. Wire ivy trails together with reel wire and position them to form a spiral effect down the cake. Place your first section of ivy so that it winds around the top tier of the cake close to the base board. Once it has circled the tier, secure the ivy to itself with some reel wire. Continue to attach more ivy trails until you have the spiral shape you desire.

2 Fill in around the base of the entire cake with larger flat ivy leaves, wiring them to the trails with stub wires. Next position the lily

heads among the ivy leaves. Wire them in place with stub wires, attaching them to the ivy stem. Place two lily heads on the top of the cake and decorate with ivy trails.

3 Next arrange the scabious flowers in the same manner. Put them in groups around the lilies and also scatter along the ivy trails.

4 Continue to build up the flower heads by wiring in the Valerie roses, white nigella and cow parsley. Last of all take the delphinium stem and cut off the single flower heads from its length. Now arrange them along with the others.

EASY LEVEL

A FLORAL CAKE

Cutting the cake is the highlight of any wedding meal and provides a chance for your arranging skills to be on show. As the moment will probably be photographed you need to keep the flowers looking good. Because the stems are not in water, complete the display quite late. Pappets could be hidden (*see p. 14*), with some moss, but the arrangement will seem heavier. Flowers also drink water through their heads so mist carefully once finished.

1

2

3

4

1 Make four holes in your candle cup, evenly placed around the sides. To do this take a stub wire and hold it over the lighted spare candle. Hold one end in the flame until it is red hot. Holding carefully, push it through the plastic candle cup at the appropriate point. The plastic will melt as the wire passes through, making a hole. Repeat for the other three holes. Next place the upturned candle cup on the florist's foam and press down. Cut around the cup shape and then wrap in chicken wire and wedge into the candle cup. Now pass a silver wire through one of the holes in the candle cup and thread it through a chicken wire strut close to the hole. Once the silver wire reaches halfway, bend it over and bring it round to meet the other end. Now twist the wires together securing the block into the candle cup. Repeat this with the other holes. Take some floral fix and use it to temporarily fix the candle cup in place in the candlestick. Leave to set. (After use remove the cup by washing away the fix with hot water.)

2 Cut a hole in the chicken wire skin around the florist's foam to allow the candle to be firmly positioned in it.

3 First cut the stems of the leatherleaf into sections to create the correct length, then arrange in the foam to form the desired shape. Fill in with large flat ivy leaves, Alchemilla mollis and eucalyptus, pushing the stems firmly into the foam. Position the ivy trails around the foam's base and trail them around the candlestick.

4 Now start inserting lily heads into the foam, then arrange the sweet pea stems. Next build up with roses and scabious. Turn your arrangement around to ensure an even floral distribution, then fill in with nigella and cow parsley flowers.

MATERIALS

(to make one decorated candlestick)

Plastic candle cup

Stub wires

Matches and spare candle

Soaked Wet florist's foam (*see p. 12*)

Scissors

Chicken wire

Silver wire

Floral fix (putty substance)

Candlestick and candle

1 bunch of leatherleaf

Some large flat ivy leaves

1 bunch each of Alchemilla mollis, eucalyptus and ivy trails

5 heads of Le Reve lilies

5 stems each of sweet peas, Valerie roses, scabious and white nigella

2 stems of cow parsley

INTERMEDIATE LEVEL

FLOWER CANDLESTICKS

Decorated candlesticks make attractive alternatives to the table arrangements normally found at wedding receptions. With the aid of a plastic cup prepared with florist's foam and inserted into the candle hole, you can instantly create a tall floral display. It will also leave space for place settings and other accessories on a small table.

You can choose between using a candelabra for three candles, placing your arrangement in the middle with one candle either side, or using a single candlestick and candle.

Make your flower arrangement with the candle cup in position in a sample of the candlestick you will be using. When complete, take it off the candlestick and pack it safely in a storage box for travelling. This will leave the candlestick free for the next arrangement.

MATERIALS

Soaked florist's foam dome with "clip" (*see p.12*)
1 bunch of leatherleaf
Scissors
1 bunch of Alchemilla mollis
1 bunch of eucalyptus
5 stems of Valerie roses
10 stems of sweet peas
3 heads of Le Reve lilies
1 bunch of scabious
1 bunch of white nigella
Silk
Pins
Chair
Plastic bag
Stub wires

ADVANCED LEVEL

DECORATED CHAIR BACKS

The backrest of a chair is an often forgotten area for flower decoration, but simple arrangements can look stunning, especially at a wedding. Before starting your design look at the chairs at the reception venue as you may need to work out how to attach the flowers. To create the design, part of a florist's foam dome with "clip" has been used, but the clip has been removed. Here, a strong wire secures the arrangement in place through the chair's woven back. Clips are normally used for decorating church pews. If it is a church wedding and you want to re-use the pew flowers, remove them after the service and attach to the chairs for the female guests at the reception, fixing the silk bows in place in advance.

1

1 Take a plastic-caged florist's foam dome with a clip attachment and remove the plastic clip. Trim the stems of leatherleaf and then insert in the foam to form the required oval shape. Let the arrangement have a drop to it so that one end will trail a little like a bridal bouquet. Then add in the Alchemilla mollis and the eucalyptus.

2 Now arrange the roses in your spray. Start with one at the centre top, at twelve o'clock, place the next rose at two o'clock with the third inserted at five o'clock. Place the next rose between seven and eight, and the last rose at nine o'clock, slightly in the background. Arrange the sweet peas randomly throughout the spray.

3 Arrange the three Le Reve lily heads deep in the spray in an offset triangular formation. Then start to fill in with some scabious flowers and the white nigella to complete the flowing style and shape of the arrangement.

4 If you're incorporating the bow, tie a length of white silk around the chair and then tie in a beautiful bow. If necessary, pin the fabric firmly in place on the chair. Cover the back of the arrangement with a section of plastic bag cut to size. This will stop any moisture soaking into the fabric or the chair. Now wire the floral arrangement onto the bow with stub wires or fix the wires through the weave of the chair back, if you are using this style.

2

3

4

1

2

3

4

TOP TABLE FLOWERS

A stunning floral arrangement on the top table at a wedding meal can be one of the most admired wedding decorations, so plan carefully, coordinating the colour of the flowers with the other floral decorations that are featured at the wedding.

Before you start the arrangement, work out the height of your design. It should not be so tall that it hides the newly married couple from view. Another point is that your flowers should look the most impressive from the front, as during the speeches all the guests will be watching the top table and the floral display will be the central attraction.

When you place the flowers on the table encourage them to trail down the front of the tablecloth. When doing this make sure that the weight of these flowers is not so heavy as to pull the rest of the arrangement off the table. Lastly, the flower arrangement should always allow enough room for each guest's place settings to be positioned with space to spare on the table.

MATERIALS

Two soaked blocks of Wet florist's foam (see p. 12), plastic tray, chicken wire, scissors, reel wire, florist's tape, 6 candles

1 bunch each of ruscus, leatherleaf, beech, flat ivy leaves

1 bunch of eucalyptus

10 stems of delphinium

2 bunches of cream stocks

10 stems of Le Reve lilies

20 stems of white nigella

10 stems each of haytor, scabious, 5 stems of cow parsley

1 bunch of Alchemilla mollis

10 stems each of Valerie roses, cream sweet peas, some ivy trails

5

6

7

8

1 Take the two foam blocks and fit them in your plastic tray and wrap in chicken wire. Use some reel wire to lace the sides of chicken wire if they do not meet, then thread some florist's tape through a chicken wire strut. Stick one end of the tape to the tray and take the other under the tray to the other side, sticking the tape to the bottom of the plastic tray as you go. Thread the free end through the wire at the other side of the tray. Repeat at either end of block.

2 Now cut holes in the chicken wire skin where you wish to place your candles. Push them firmly

into the foam through the new holes in the chicken wire. Six candles have been inserted along this display, some in groups, some alone.

3 Now start to arrange the foliage. First insert the ruscus, positioning a length at each end of the floral block to define the display's length. Continue to form the shape you want by adding in the leatherleaf and the beech, using long and shorter stems. Add in the flat ivy leaves randomly to give some extra texture. Then insert long and shorter stems of eucalyptus to cover all of the foam block.

4 Insert one stem of delphinium, following the lines of the ruscus, at each end of the arrangement. Arrange more stems of delphinium at the sides, allowing them to cascade down the front. Position more stems throughout the top section. Next arrange the stocks through the front.

5 Place lilies at each end of the arrangement, slightly shorter in length than the delphiniums. Insert more randomly along the shape.

6 Next add in the nigella, haytor and scabious flowers with the shorter stems. Arrange them so that

they trail down the front, also put them deep in the foliage and through the top section.

7 Fill out the areas that require it with cow parsley and Alchemilla mollis to add more of a frothy texture to the design.

8 Now to finish, scatter some roses throughout, placing them so that they are shown to their best advantage. Fill out any dead spots with cream sweet peas to create a delicate effect. Once the display is in its final position on the top table, insert some ivy trails .

A JARDINIÈRE DISPLAY

As table space at weddings is often at a premium, a jardinière arrangement is an ideal choice because it is tall enough to thrust its floral display high into the air, clearing the level of the guests' heads so that they can still talk to each other across the table. This design should only be used at the tables set toward the edges of the reception room to make sure that everyone has a clear view of the bride and groom.

If the room has a period feel, this will be echoed beautifully by the style of this arrangement. Flowers in abundance have been loosely arranged and cascade out of the basket at the top of the jardinière, creating a romantic, intimate atmosphere underneath. This design has been developed to give strong visual impact and will be an important feature at the wedding celebration. If you do not want to use it as a beautiful table arrangement, as shown here, it will make an attractive free-standing decoration at the reception or at the church.

Once again, as with all the other projects featured in this section, the design can also be scaled down to suit your needs and your budget.

MATERIALS

Jardinière (available from garden centres)
Carpet moss
5 ivy plants
Plastic freezer bags
Stub wires
Plastic container
A large chicken wire wrap with Wet florist's foam (*see p. 12*)
Reel wire
Scissors
2 long-stemmed bunches each of beech, ruscus and eucalyptus
10 stems of delphiniums
10 stems of Le Reve lilies
10 stems of cow parsley
2 bunches each of cream and white stocks
20 stems of Valerie roses
1 bunch of Alchemilla mollis

1 Start constructing the jardinière arrangement on site and only lift it into its place on the table once it is completed. First start to line the jardinière's basket with sections of carpet moss, still leaving plenty of room inside the basket.

2 Take some well-watered ivy plants and divide them up into smaller sizes, keeping the root systems intact. Wrap the root balls in plastic freezer bags to stop the roots from drying out and fasten the top of each bag with a stub wire. Next position them around the basket area, pushing the bags right through the moss wall. The moss will keep the ivy bags in place. Next place all the chicken wire wrapped foam blocks upright on their ends in the plastic container.

3 Insert the plastic container in the basket on top of the moss and fill in with more moss if necessary. Wire the container securely into the basket with reel wire. Attach lengths of reel wire around the chicken wire holding the florist's foam in the

1

2

3

4

5

6

7

8

plastic container and attach them to the struts of the basket.

4 Arrange the beech, ruscus and eucalyptus mixed foliage in the foam to form a shape that radiates out from the middle of the basket. Use all the foliage in lengths as long as possible, so that you create an explosive, dramatic feel to the floral arrangement. Allow the natural fall of the ruscus to follow the lines of the trailing ivy.

5 Now start to insert five of the delphinium stems, radiating them like wheel spokes from the edge of the basket. Arrange the stems horizontally from the foam and let the weight of the stems pull the ends down to echo the fall of the ruscus. Next arrange a group of three delphiniums as though they were shooting out from the top of the arrangement. Arrange the remaining two delphiniums deeper in the sides of the arrangement. Make sure that the top three are visible from all sides of the jardinière.

6 Start to arrange the Le Reve lilies, placing one stem in the middle at the top to give more height. Place more lilies throughout the design until they are evenly distributed throughout.

7 Add in stems of cow parsley to give a frothy feel. Next insert the shorter stems of the cream and white stocks deep in the foliage to give the arrangement some background and added depth.

8 Place the Valerie roses to look as though they have been randomly scattered among all the other flowers. Group some together and place others individually. Stand back and take a look at the arrangement and then fill in any noticeable holes with some stems of Alchemilla mollis.

VALENTINE'S DAY

What better way to celebrate this most romantic of days than with a candlelit dinner for two. Start by setting an informal table, placing the chairs close together to create a relaxed, intimate atmosphere. Make sure that you choose an easily prepared menu that will only take moments to serve. And don't forget to have plenty of champagne on ice to add to the evening's pleasure.

Red roses have represented love ever since the days of the early Greeks, and increasing numbers are now sold each year on Valentine's Day to romantics of all ages.

To avoid disappointment when buying your roses from a florist, place your order a few days before and arrange a convenient collection time.

Develop your romantic theme using glasses, a dinner service and a tablecloth and napkins that will tone in with your designs and table setting.

1

2

3

4

1 Cut the first rose down close to the head, but don't throw away the stem and leaves. With a thick stub wire pierce the stem close to the flower and then push the wire through about one-third of the way.

2 Bend both parts of the wire downward and then wrap the shorter stem twice around the flower's stem before twisting it together firmly with the longer wire.

3 Wind some gutta around the stem as close to the flower head as possible. Twist it around tightly, travelling downward as you cover all

the wire and start to create a new stem for the rose.

4 Cut two sets of leaves off the reserved stem and place the first set onto the false stem of the rose. Cover with the gutta, attaching it firmly to the false stem. Continue covering the false stem until you reach the end. Position the second set of rose leaves further down the stem and attach them using exactly the same method. To finish, wind the finished wire stem around a freshly laundered napkin. Repeat this method to make up the second rose napkin ring for your dinner partner.

MATERIALS
(to make two napkin rings)
2 Nicole roses
Scissors
Thick stub wires
Gutta tape or stemwind
2 freshly laundered napkins

ROSE NAPKIN RINGS

The method you employ to make these appealing Valentine's napkin holders is very similar to the one you would use to make a rose buttonhole to wear for a wedding. The only difference is the extension of the wire and the additional leaves that are incorporated into this romantic design.

As the roses will spend the evening out of water, make sure that they are well conditioned by giving them a good "drink" before you cut them down to size. Make the project at the last possible moment and give the roses a generous spray with a water mister when they are finished.

The gutta used to cover the wire on the napkin rings is an old-fashioned paper type that helps lend texture to the design. More modern versions are available, but are made from plastic and tend to give a more artificial feel.

The napkin holders will need a thicker gauge wire than you might normally use for a normal buttonhole as the wire needs to be strong enough to hold the napkin firmly in place.

71

ROSE CANDLE HOLDER

This pretty candle holder makes a stunning centrepiece that helps to add that extra touch of romance to your Valentine's Day meal. The method of decorating the candle is different from the Flower Candlesticks that were featured in the Wedding section (*see pp. 58–59*) as this first method relied on a candle cup to produce the finished floral display. The second method shown here uses pappets, disguised by moss, to keep the roses fresh and watered. This means that you can make the project up to a day in advance as the pappets can be easily topped up with water. And there is a further advantage to this method – fresh, seasonal flowers can then be used to replace the original rose heads and extend the life of the arrangement well after Valentine's Day has passed.

MATERIALS

| 1 candlestick |
| 5 pappets filled with water |
| (*see p.14*) |
| Moss |
| Candle |
| Florist's tape |
| A reel of silver wire |
| 7 stems of Nicole roses |
| 1 bunch of ivy trails |

1 Select the candlestick that you are using for this project and tape all the filled pappets onto it at staggered intervals all the way up.

2 Wind moss around the candlestick in a spiral fashion and bind it in place with a reel of silver wire. Remember to leave some spaces clear for the tops of the pappets to show through.

3 Cut the stems of the roses close to the heads, leaving them just long enough to reach the bottom of the pappets. Push the stems into the fixed pappets, arranging the rose heads in position, all the way up the candlestick.

4 To finish the decoration, twist some ivy trails around the candlestick so that the ivy gives the appearance of naturally growing up the candlestick's length. Wire the ivy firmly into position with the silver wire. Place the candle in the holder and light it when your meal is ready and your guest is sitting at the table. Top up the pappets daily with some water to make sure that the roses give you a long-lasting display.

1

2

3

4

MOTHER'S DAY

Breakfast in bed is always a real treat, and it has become a tradition in many households for children to prepare their mother's breakfast on Mother's Day. Making a special mat to go on her tray will be a surprise in itself, but adding a decorated napkin ring or a flower posy will really delight the mother and make a wonderful start to her day.

The projects that have been chosen for the Mother's Day section have been especially worked out so that children can also make them. In theory, each idea can be made without an adult's supervision. However, if any assistance is found to be necessary (for example, if the child is very young or has not studied sewing at school), the child can seek the help of an aunt or another relative so that their treat is kept as a complete surprise for the special day.

EASY LEVEL

A BREAKFAST TRAY MAT

This simple idea makes an ideal gift for Mother's Day that will be treasured by every recipient. The mat decorates a tray beautifully and can be used throughout the year as a reminder of that special day when it was first given. It can be hand- or machine-sewn, and is easily made from a fabric remnant. If you don't have any suitable material at home, you should be able to find a piece this size in the remnant section at your fabric store, at a local market or alternatively in a discounted fabric shop.

1

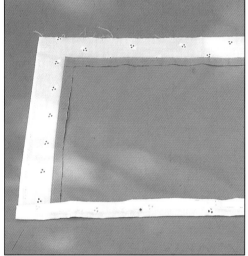

2

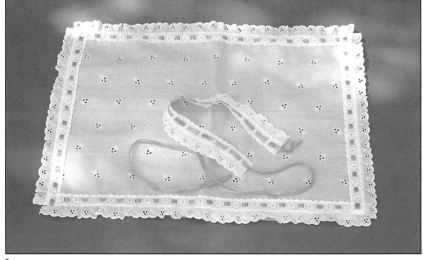

3

74

1 Cut out a piece of blue cotton fabric to measurements that are slightly larger than the tray that is being used for the mat. Next cut out the broiderie anglaise to make a shape that is slightly larger than the first piece.

2 Fold down and pin a hem all around the blue fabric of about 1in (2.5cm). Check that the piece will now fit the size of your tray and then place with the hem facing upward on top of the broiderie anglaise material. Fold down the broiderie anglaise material over the blue material to make a double hem of about 2 in (5cm) and pin this in place. Lightly baste all the way around this double hem, removing all the pins as you sew.

3 Cut your broiderie anglaise edging into four pieces to match the length of the four sides of the mat and then thread through the blue ribbon. Neaten ends by turning in, then pin and lightly baste all the edging pieces into position on the right side of the mat as shown. To finish, hand stitch or machine sew them onto the tray mat, going through all the material layers, and then remove all the basting stitches.

MATERIALS
1 high-sided tray
Blue cotton fabric
Dressmaking scissors
White broiderie anglaise fabric
Pins
Needle and thread or sewing machine
Broiderie anglaise edging
Blue ribbon

A RAFFIA NAPKIN RING

This pretty napkin ring can also be added to your breakfast tray for the surprise breakfast. It provides a special and lasting Mother's Day gift that will always be greatly treasured. It can also be used afterward at any dinner party table setting.

The ring itself, hand-covered with blue raffia, makes a lovely present just as it is, but you can also go on to dec-orate it further with some fresh or dried flowers. By gluing fresh flower heads of your choice onto a length of broiderie anglaise or leftover material you can attach flowers to the napkin ring and then, once they have died, remove and discard them, or replace them with some fresh ones from the garden or florist.

If you prefer to add a more perma-nent decoration to the napkin ring, use some dried flower heads instead. To achieve the attractive effect that is shown here a combination of both fresh spray roses and also sweet-smelling dried lavender was used on the finished napkin ring.

1

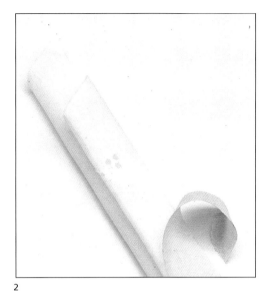

2

3

4

MATERIALS

1 wooden napkin ring
Blue raffia
A piece of broiderie anglaise
Tape
Dressmaking scissors
Strong glue or hot glue gun
Scissors
1 spray of roses, cut to size
Dried lavender sprigs

1 Take the wooden napkin ring and bind the blue raffia around it until it is completely covered. Hold the loose ends and tie together.

2 Make a band out of the broiderie anglaise material by folding a length over and over until you have a thick enough band to take the glue. Tape the final edge of the fabric into place.

3 Wrap the band around the napkin ring until the two ends overlap on the inside of the ring and then cut it to size. Glue the ends together with a strong glue or a hot

glue gun. Cut the spray roses to size and then use the glue again to secure them firmly in position on the broiderie anglaise band.

4 Finally glue the dried lavender sprigs in place on the band to complete the decoration and add a sweet-smelling aroma to your finished napkin ring.

1 Take your glass vase and cut out enough of the blue cotton and broiderie anglaise fabrics to cover it fully. Place the broiderie anglaise face down and then put the blue cotton fabric face down on top of it. Place the glass vase in the middle of the two layers of fabric.

2 Now gather up the layers together around the container and, holding the fabrics in one hand, tie a length of blue ribbon to secure the fabric firmly at the neck of the glass vase.

3 Cut the legs of the ribbon to size, or tie in a bow if you prefer. Now roll the fabric up, twisting it around the neck of the glass vase. Start and finish this roll at the back of the vase.

4 Once the roll is completed tuck in the loose ends and pin the roll to hold it firmly in place.

5 Carefully fill the vase with water, leaving enough room at the top to allow for any movement. Cut the stems of senecio to the length you require, and arrange them in the vase. Then take a bunch of dried lavender and arrange the stems together in clumps throughout the floral posy to add further aroma.

6 Take the bunch of fragrant white freesias and add them to the vase, arranging them carefully. Next cut down the roses from the larger stem of the spray and display them in the vase to complete this special posy.

1

2

3

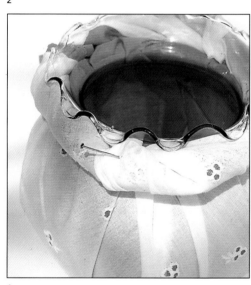

4

5

6

A SCENTED FLORAL POSY

A fresh flower posy will always be received with surprise and delight on Mother's Day, but when it is combined with a special breakfast in bed the appreciation will be doubled.

Always use highly fragrant flowers to make up the posy. The spray roses that have been chosen here have a beautiful scent and freesias are renowned for their individual perfume. The dried lavender in this posy can also be kept afterward and perhaps used to freshen a drawer full of clothes with its delicate smell.

The covered vase is very simple and quick to make. It is covered in blue cotton and broiderie anglaise material to match the tray mat project (*see pp. 74–75*). As there is no sewing involved, this cover can be quickly removed when the vase needs to be cleaned and then put on again with the minimum of fuss.

MATERIALS
1 glass vase
Dressmaking scissors
Blue cotton fabric to cover vase
Broiderie anglaise to cover vase
Blue ribbon
Pin
Scissors
1 bunch of senecio
1 bunch of dried lavender
1 bunch of white freesias
1 spray of roses

FESTIVALS

CHRISTMAS

Christmas is still the favourite time of year for many people, when family and friends can gather together to celebrate the festival. It brings with it such a host of old, established traditions for decorations and the materials that are used to make them. Long-lasting seasonal foliage such as blue pine and holly have been used in the featured Christmas table arrangement and always make a good foundation to build upon. By adding in walnuts, cinnamon sticks and festive ribbons you really make an eye-catching display.

If you don't feel up to making the more complicated large hanging wreath, first attempt the simple candle project that looks extremely attractive but does not demand too many decorating skills.

The Victorians introduced many of the Christmas traditions that are still used today. In fact, their influence has structured all our festivities. This view has inspired the period-style designs of these seasonal projects and helps to give them a warm, nostalgic look.

EASY LEVEL

FESTIVE CANDLES

Candles have featured strongly in the projects in this book. The soft light they give out instantly creates a warm, atmospheric setting. They can also add to the sense of occasion and when Christmas arrives the candle can stand as a symbol of purity, peace and goodwill. An advantage of this simple candle design is that you can use several candles, but do not have to invest in any candlesticks.

When candles are alight, never let them burn too close to the decoration, keep young children away and do not leave them unattended.

1

2

3

MATERIALS
3 large, thick white candles
Floral fix
1 medium terracotta saucer
Bun moss
Glue (optional)
Dark green wired ribbon
Scissors
Silver wire

1 Take the three white candles and spread some floral fix onto the base of each one. Press each candle firmly into position on the terracotta saucer and then hold in place for a short time until the floral fix bonds the two surfaces together. (After use the floral fix can be washed away under hot water.)

2 Next fill in the gap around the sides of the saucer and the candles with some bun moss, wedging it firmly in position. If you prefer you could also glue the moss onto the container for extra stability.

3 Take a length of the dark green ribbon and form a bow shape with it (*see p. 15*), first gathering the ribbon together in one hand at the centre. Once you have made the bow you can wire it together with silver wire to hold it in position. Finally, tie a length of ribbon around the base of all three candles, then tie the pre-made bow into position on top. Keep experimenting with primping the ribbon into shape until you are completely happy with its finished appearance.

INTERMEDIATE LEVEL

CRACKERS

MATERIALS
(to make one cracker)

Scissors

1 large sheet of red
handmade paper

1 A4 sheet of plain, thick card

1 cracker bang

1 Victorian reproduction
party mask

1 cardboard tube

Strong glue or hot glue gun

Cord or raffia

Gifts

Tartan ribbon

Small piece of tartan silk

Crackers are a favourite for every Christmas table, but they can also be used at other times during the year, especially when you would like to give a gift to your guests at a dinner party.

Adapt your Christmas crackers to the size you want using the method detailed on the next page. They can be small enough to be included in swagging, or as large as the jumbo crackers shown here containing novelty gifts and a reproduction Victorian party mask as an alternative to a paper hat.

The crackers have been made from a rich-textured handmade paper and are decorated with the tartan silk and ribbon used in the other projects in this section. If you prefer, choose some fabric or paper cutouts that will complement the theme of your table to embellish your crackers.

This is an ideal project to make with the help of your children – either in the half-term holiday or during the busy run-up to Christmas Day. You can keep the crackers' novelties a secret by popping them inside once the children have gone to bed.

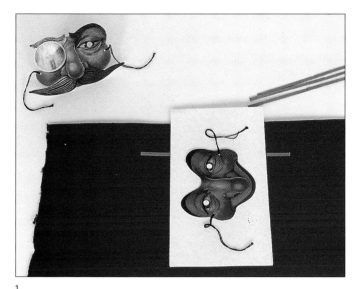

1

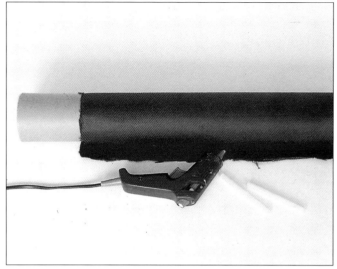

2

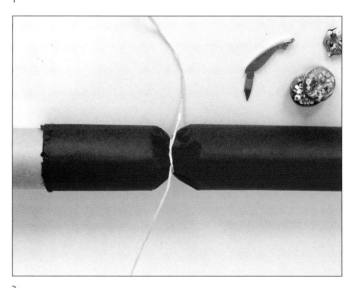

3

4

1 Cut the red handmade paper, or the paper you have chosen to form the cracker, to the size you require, roughly working it out first on some scrap paper. The one detailed here is jumbo size. Now cut some thick card to the size you wish the body of the cracker to be – it's normally about a third of the size of the cracker paper – and put it in the middle. Place it so that its edge overlaps the paper at the top. Slip in the cracker bang and the party mask.

2 Now take a long cardboard tube and place it along the top edge of the paper and roll the red paper around the tube. The overlapping edge of the card will ensure that the body is round. Once you have rolled the paper around the tube completely, glue the paper's edges in place with a strong glue or with a hot glue gun. Leave the glue to dry for a short time.

3 Now ease the tube slowly out of the paper roll, keeping the card in place inside until only about a quarter is left. The end of the tube is now positioned so that it forms the required length of the cracker handle. Then tie some cord around the paper at the point between the edge of the tube and the edge of the card inside the cracker body. Remove the cardboard tube, turn the open end of the cracker upward and carefully drop all your chosen gifts right into the body of the cracker. Repeat the tying procedure with the cord at the other end of the cracker body so that you form the second cracker handle.

4 Cut lengths of the tartan ribbon to a similar length as both the cords and tie them into bows (see p. 15) at each end of the cracker to disguise the cords. Glue some strips of ribbon in place around each end of the cracker, then decorate the main body of the cracker with a strip of tartan silk and glue it firmly into place. Following the same method, make as many other crackers as you think you are likely to need over the busy festive period.

1

2

3

4

MATERIALS

FROSTED FRUIT

1 egg
2 bowls
Pastry brush
Fruit such as grapes, pears or redcurrants
Colander
1 tablespoon
Granulated sugar

CHOCOLATE COCONUTS

1 bar of cooking chocolate
1 bowl
A pan of hot water
1 tablespoon
1 bag of miniature coconuts
1 plate

1 To make the frosted fruit, first separate the white of an egg from the yolk over a bowl. Put the yolk in the other bowl, and with a pastry brush coat your chosen fruit with egg white. Apply the egg white sparingly to the fruit. To coat a lot of fruit, separate more eggs as needed

2 Place a colander over a large bowl. Position the prepared fruit in the colander and with the tablespoon sprinkle a liberal amount of granulated sugar over the fruit. Put the fruit to one side until set. Once the sugar has hardened completely, the fruit is ready to use.

3 To make the miniature chocolate coconuts, first melt the bar of cooking chocolate in a bowl over a pan of hot water. Once the chocolate has melted completely, remove from the heat. Alternatively, you can melt the chocolate in an oven-proof bowl for about 50 seconds on High in the microwave.

4 Stir some miniature coconuts into the bowl until they are covered in the melted chocolate, then place them carefully on a plate to set. Serve them straightaway with some coffee or store them away in an airtight tin until they are needed.

FROSTED FRUIT AND CHOCOLATE NUTS

The beauty of this frosted fruit is that it makes a superb decoration for your table, whether skilfully arranged on a raised fruit dish as a centrepiece or included in flower arrangements. The fruit is deliciously fresh and light to eat after the heavy texture of the traditional Christmas pudding.

The frosting on the fruit is evocative of the wintry weather of the season as it dries to a crisp, hard coating reminiscent of ice. Make sure that you prepare the fruit well before you need to use it, as the coating will take some time to set. You do not want the syrupy covering running over and possibly spoiling your polished table surface.

Miniature coconuts complete with shell have been used for the second part of this project. Once covered in the melted chocolate they make a tasty bite to serve with coffee. If you can't buy the miniature coconuts, you can also use small fresh or dried fruits, shelled nuts or coffee beans.

ADVANCED LEVEL

SEASONAL TABLE FEATURE

This project using winter foliage, flowers and decorations is infinitely adaptable and can be made to suit any requirements. The shape can easily be altered because no container is used and the foliage and flowers are arranged directly onto plastic sheeting laid out to protect your table. This allows you the freedom to decorate as much or as little of your table as you wish.

This design also uses two of the other projects in this section. The Festive Candles from pages 82–83 feature prominently in the arrangement, and the Frosted Fruit from pages 86–87 are used with cinnamon sticks, flowers, ribbons, gold stars and walnuts to decorate the run of mixed Christmas foliage to perfection.

Pappets (*see p. 14*) can be used in this project to keep the flowers from wilting. They will also enable you to decorate the table well in advance and make your table centrepiece last during the holiday period. Make sure that the pappets are topped up daily, and that the flowers are replaced regularly.

1

2

3

4

1 Place some plastic bin bags over the area of the table you wish to decorate. This will help protect your table surface from any scratches from the rough foliage stems or from any water leakage from the pappets. If you wish, cover the plastic with an absorbent cloth as an extra precaution. Judge how big you want the table feature and then cut the blue pine branches to the desired size and place them on the covering. Now cut some sprigs of holly and distribute them along the blue pine, weaving their stems into the fingers of the pine. Then arrange the ivy in the pine using this same method.

2 Position the three sets of Festive Candles on the pine run of foliage. Cut bark pieces to size and decorate some of the pine with them. Next arrange the cinnamon sticks in the pine.

3 Take some of the prepared Frosted Fruit and lay it on the pine base. Cluster the fruit together in groups and also arrange some of the fruit individually all along the run of foliage.

4 Spray some walnuts and the undersides of pine cones with gold paint and allow to dry, then arrange them along with the gold star decorations among the fruit. Cut the Vicky Brown roses down to size and place their stems in pappets filled with water. Do the same with the large white Oriental lily heads and arrange them throughout the fruit and foliage run. Make large festive bows (see p. 15) from the tartan ribbon and place them in the foliage to complete the look of the table decoration.

MATERIALS

(to decorate one chair back)

1 wire wreath frame

Reel wire

Sphagnum moss

Scissors

1 large bunch of blue pine

Stub wires

1 bag of mini pine cones

1 bunch of variegated holly

1 bag of walnuts

Gold spray paint

1 bag of gold star decorations

Tartan ribbon

Tartan silk

Plastic bin liner

1

2

1 Take the wreath frame and attach the end of some reel wire to a strut by twisting the wire around it. Next take some sphagnum moss and bind it onto the frame with the reel wire. Build up with moss until the frame is covered. Leave reel wire attached to frame.

2 Cut all the blue pine to size and remove the needles from the ends of the stems. Push the stems into the moss on the wreath in the same direction and, with the reel wire, bind them into position.

3

4

3 Wind stub wires around the bottom of some pine cones and push the wire legs through the pine and moss on the wreath. Open them out on the other side, then return the ends back into the moss. Attach all the pine cones randomly to the wreath. Next cut the holly to size and remove some leaves from the stems. Push these into the moss.

4 Spray some walnuts with gold paint and leave to dry. Take a thick stub wire and bend it in half. Insert the rounded end into the soft end of the walnut, between the crack at the bottom. Push the stub wire legs through the wreath frame and attach in the same way as the pine cones. Take the gold stars and attach with more stub wires. Next make bows (*see p. 15*) out of the ribbon, wrap stub wires around them and wire onto the wreath.

(*see p. 15*)

ADVANCED LEVEL

HOLLY AND PINE CHAIR BACKS

Once you've chosen the design for your Christmas table you can consider decorating your dining chairs, if you have suitable chair backs. The chair used here had a carved central strut which made it easy to wire the wreath onto it.

If you are unable to use this project for your dining room, then try making the wreath for your front door.

5

5 Finally, tie a sash of tartan silk around the chair back and pin into place. Attach strips of plastic bin liner to the back of the wreath to protect against the damp moss. Next attach two lengths of reel wire to the wreath frame, one at the top and one at the bottom. Attach to chair by winding the wires around the central strut, twist ends together, then cut off excess wire. Decorate other dining chairs in the same way.

HANGING WREATH

This advent wreath can be a superb way of decorating your dining room during the festivities as it can be suspended from a secure hook in the ceiling or a crossbeam over your table.

Most of the Christmas foliage that has been used should last through the holiday. The blue pine survives well, but the holly may need replacing. Add lilies just before Christmas Day to heighten the sense of occasion.

The wreath can be made smaller as the wire frame is available in several sizes. Always make sure that its weight is no heavier than its hook will allow.

MATERIALS
1 large wire wreath frame
Reel wire
Scissors
Gold metal chain, cut to length (from DIY store)
Stub wires
Sphagnum moss
4 bunches of blue pine, cut to size
A bunch of cupressus, cut to size
1 bag each of large and small pine cones
Gold spray paint
Cinnamon sticks
Gold sun, moon and star decorations
Candles
3–4 stems of Oriental white lilies, cut to short stems
Pappets (see p. 14)

1 Take the wreath frame and mark four quarters along the inside – some will already have four struts. Take some reel wire and wind around each strut or quarter, cut, then twist the wire legs together. Take the chain strips and attach one end to each quarter wire. Slip the last link over the wire legs and twist legs together, then wire all four ends together with a thick stub wire to form a loop.

2 Tie the reel wire to one strut. Next add moss to cover the frame and bind with the wire, leaving it attached.

3 Remove pine needles from bottom of the the blue pine's stems. Push a sprig into the moss and bind with the wire, then insert all of them in the same direction, binding them with reel wire as you proceed, until the wreath is covered. Turn over and cover the underside using the same method. Insert the cupressus between the pine in the same way, then cut the reel wire and secure firmly.

4 Gild the underside of the pine cones with gold paint, leaving some natural. Fix randomly throughout the frame by winding stub wires onto the cones (*see p. 14*), pushing the legs through the frame and opening them out on the other side, then returning the ends back into the moss.

5 Next insert cinnamon sticks using the same method as pine cones, following the foliage. Attach stub wires to the holes in the gold decorations and secure onto wreath.

6 Lastly secure four candles to the frame. To fix, take a thick stub wire and hold over a flame. Once the wire is red hot, insert it into the candle's base. The hot end will melt the wax, allowing the wire to be pushed in. Carefully insert three or four wires, next push the other ends of the wires through the wreath frame and pull firmly so that the candle sits well. Then tuck the wires back up through to the top, bend back and secure. (Warning: never leave lit candles unattended.) Secure the wreath to the ceiling hook with the stub wire loop (see Step 1). Just before Christmas Day place the lilies in pappets and wedge carefully in between the foliage.

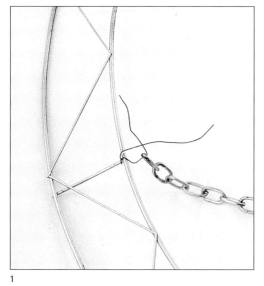

1

2

3

4

5

6

NEW YEAR

This table setting, with its clean lines and subtle sophistication, has been devised to give you a fresh start to the New Year after all the fuss and trimmings of Christmas. The effect has been achieved by creating a modern look in black and white and adding a touch of deep burgundy. The dinner service also follows this colour scheme by using large black underplates to set off to stunning effect the white and silver plates and bowls. A final flourish is added to the style of the table by the dramatic floral display, which gives some extra contrast and texture to the table layout.

Carrying your chosen colour scheme through to the menu can also be fun, and will almost certainly impress the dinner guests around your table, but always make sure that the food still looks appetizing.

Changing all your table linen to suit new colour themes is just not a practical option. So with this project use a neutral tablecloth as a background, and highlight your place settings with the personalized napkins and the fun party hats.

Once again, candlelight has been used to enhance the layout. Here, night lights in frosted glass containers have been scattered along the table to provide a warm background glow without being too obtrusive.

EASY LEVEL

PRINTED NAPKINS

A novel way to bring the New Year you are celebrating into your table design is with this simple project. The black napkins used for this setting have been potato-printed with the date of both the outgoing old year and the incoming new one. The use of a subtle metallic silver paint on the black material has meant that the design has stayed in keeping with the rest of the table's colour scheme.

MATERIALS
(to print one napkin)
Large potatoes
Long sharp knife
Pastry number cutters
Silver metallic fabric paint
Paintbrush
Black napkin
Iron

1 Take a potato and cut a thin slice off the top of the flattest area. Place the appropriate number-shaped pastry cutter onto the cut potato and make sure that it is in reverse. Insert the pastry cutter into the potato by upturning it and pushing it down onto a hard surface. Keep pushing down until the cutter edge is level with the potato's surface. Now slice off a layer of the potato to reveal the sides of the pastry cutter. Remove the pastry cutter from the potato.

2 Paint the protruding shape liberally with the silver metallic fabric paint. Keep the edges clear from clots of paint as these could easily blot the printed number.

3 Spread out the black napkin and turn the potato upside down, positioning the number on the cloth. Press down for a moment, then remove the potato. Repeat these steps until you have printed the date of the New Year and the Old Year. Leave the printed napkin overnight to dry, then firmly seal the paint with a hot iron the next day, following the manufacturer's instructions. Make all the other napkins in the same way, then wash and press them in readiness for your New Year party.

1

2

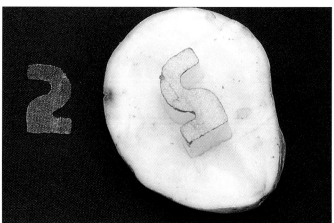

3

PARTY HATS

A New Year's dinner party should be fun and making party hats to suit the occasion will add to the frivolity. Use the same colour scheme as for the table settings, but also feature the essence of New Year – its arrival at twelve o'clock midnight – by making movable clock hands as part of the hats' design. They are easy to make using cutouts of stiff card layered together to provide reinforcement so that the hats will last throughout the evening's revelries.

1 Mark out clock shape on back of cards using soup and side plates for curves. Cut out two shapes from the black and one from silver card.

2 Then using the side plate mark out the areas to be cut away on the black shapes to reveal the silver card underneath forming the clock face.

Cut out the clock hands from the remaining black card, then glue a grip binder onto the big hand and punch a hole into the small hand's end.

3 Cut elastic to fit an average head and staple ends together. To form the hat's back section, take one black shape and cut two slits about 6in (1.5cm) apart to make a tab in the base. Put elastic under this and staple.

4 Cut side plate hole out of other black clock shape to form front. Glue the silver clock shape underneath for the clock face. In its centre make a hole with scissors, then thread a silver grip binder washer onto the grip binder's legs on the big hand. Slip on small hand, thread legs through the clock face hole, and open. Push flat, adjust time, and glue black card shape with elastic in place for the hat's back.

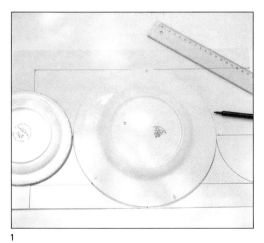

1

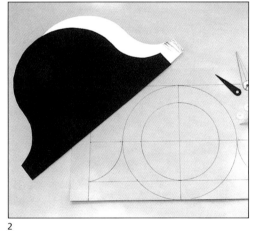

2

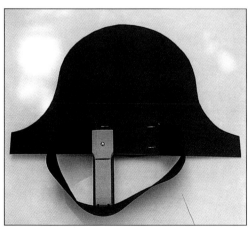

3

4

MATERIALS
(to make one hat)
1 sheet each of thick black and silver card
1 soup plate
1 side plate
Pen or pencil
Ruler
Scissors
Silver grip binder
Hole punch
Thick elastic strip
Stapler
Glue or hot glue gun

MATERIALS

1 large and 1 small freezerproof glass bowl
1 bottle of still mineral water
Scissors
1 bunch of green nigella, cut to size
5 stems of phlox, cut to size
5 stems of Escimo white roses with petals removed
1 punnet of blackcurrants
1 bag of red kidney beans or weights
1 plastic bag

INTERMEDIATE LEVEL

AN ICE BOWL

This method of serving a chilled course is attractive and functional. Flowers, berries and foliages can be frozen in the bowl to provide a unusual decoration to your table, and the ice will keep a starter or dessert cold .

Whatever you freeze in the ice will be preserved until the bowl melts. This means that you can freeze some summer flowers, store the bowl in the freezer, then bring it out onto your table in winter to add an unexpected reminder of summer.

1

2

1 Take the glass bowls and check the sizes carefully as one needs to sit easily inside the other. Almost half fill the larger bowl with still mineral water. Then add the nigella, phlox, rose petals and blackcurrants, and stir together. Next fill the smaller bowl with the kidney beans or add in the weights.

2 Place the weighted smaller bowl into the water of the larger bowl and adjust the weights so that it floats correctly. Top up with mineral water if necessary. Place both bowls overnight in a freezer compartment. The next day check to see if the water has completely frozen. Just before the bowl is required for use run hot tap water over the bowls to loosen them. Then take out the small bowl, remove the ice bowl and place on a plate. Stand The ice bowl on a small piece of plastic bag to stop it from sliding around. Decorate the bowl with some crushed ice, fill with the desired starter or pudding course and serve to your guests.

1

2

3

4

PARTY FLOWERS

The contemporary feel to this table setting is really enhanced by its stunning centrepiece. The clean lines of the glass tank container echo those of the rest of the table perfectly, and the gray eucalyptus and bear grass blend in with the silver of the dinner service. The Oriental flavour lent by the exotic orchids just accentuates the stylized look. Plain glass marbles anchor the flowers in position.

MATERIALS
1 glass tank vase

2 bags of plain glass marbles

Water

Scissors

1 bunch of eucalyptus

4 stems of Cymbidium orchids

1 bunch of bear grass

1 Take the glass tank vase and half fill it with clear glass marbles and water.

2 Next cut the eucalyptus stems to size and remove all the leaves that would normally go under the waterline. Arrange the eucalyptus like the spokes of a wheel radiating from the middle of the glass vase. Insert the stems firmly into the marbles, wedging them in place.

3 Cut the long stems of the orchids in half, and then arrange them in the marbles. Fill in with more eucalyptus, arranging the stems upright in the middle of the vase to give the arrangement more height.

4 Cut lengths of bear grass to size and then arrange them in clumps throughout the eucalyptus and the orchids. Place the tank vase on the table and top up water.

EASTER

Whether you celebrate Easter as a religious festival or just view it as a holiday weekend, it still marks a turning point of the year and heralds the arrival of spring.

An afternoon tea with sandwiches and homemade cakes presents a relaxed and casual way to entertain a gathering of family and friends for an hour or two. Young, boisterous children will love being sent off to run freely on an Easter egg hunt to find the painted eggs that you've made.

EASY LEVEL

PAINTED EGGS

These handpainted eggs make a simple yet effective table decoration when arranged in a basket or bowl. They can also be given to people as small Easter tokens. It is very easy to "blow" the eggs, but it can take stamina. You may want to prepare them over some weeks. Try blowing one or two eggs when you need them for cooking. The method of emptying the shell is a bit unhygienic, so only use the egg mixture for your own consumption.

1

MATERIALS
(to make one painted egg)
1 egg
Pin
Bowl
Sticky star shapes
Gold spray paint
Red spray paint
Black poster paint
Cloth
Glass beads and gold ornaments
Strong glue

1 Make a hole in either end of an egg with a pin, piercing the yolk inside. Hold over a bowl and blow hard through one hole – the egg will soon flow out of the other end into the bowl. Once the egg is empty, rinse it under a tap and dry. Arrange sticky star shapes on the shell or spray with gold paint and leave to dry.

2 Take the star-decorated egg and spray on a covering of red paint; leave to dry. For the gold egg rub on some black paint with a cloth and polish off to leave a burnished effect.

3 Now decorate the gold egg with glass beads and gold ornaments stuck on with strong glue, or for the other egg remove the sticky star shapes to reveal the natural eggshell.

2

3

1

2

3

4

MATERIALS

Plastic container

Soaked Wet florist's foam (*see p. 12*) or Springtime variety

Knife

Moss

1 large and 3 small baskets with handles

Reel wire, scissors

1 bunch each of leatherleaf, golden privet, Arum lilies, white spray roses, cut to size

10 stems of alstroemeria

2 bunches of yellow freesias

1 spray of daisy chrysanthemums

2 bags of mini chocolate eggs

1 Take a plastic container that will easily fit into your large basket and prepare it with the florist's foam. Cut the foam to size and wedge it firmly inside the container. Place the prepared container in the basket and keep it in place with handfuls of moss. Next use sections of the reel wire to fix the three small baskets onto the handle of the large basket or onto its rim.

2 Start to arrange the leatherleaf and golden privet stems in the florist's foam, radiating the foliage upward and out to the side from a centre point in the container.

3 Now take all the Arum lilies and arrange them carefully in a triangular formation in the basket. Next place the smaller white spray roses in the display, inserting them randomly throughout the basket.

4 Continue to add the spray roses until they are spaced throughout the basket. Next insert the alstroemeria, cut down to size, in the same manner as the roses. Add in some warmth and colour by inserting the yellow freesias into the arrangement, cutting them down a bit if necessary. Try to dot them around the other pale flowers in the basket. Now cut daisy chrysanthemum heads off the main stem, leaving their individual stems as long as possible. Push the flower stems deep into the basket to give some background and depth to the whole arrangement. Finally, finish off the seasonal display by filling up the small baskets with some mini chocolate Easter eggs and then place the flowers on the tea table ready for friends and family.

A SPRING FLORAL BASKET

These beautiful spring flowers can be used as a central table decoration for an Easter afternoon tea.

Around the large basket of the flower arrangement smaller baskets have been wired into position. These contain mini chocolate eggs which children will delight in raiding.

If you do use all spring cut flowers for your arrangement, you might like to use a softer florist's foam to accommodate their soft stems. A Springtime variety is available from sundry floral stockists. If you still have difficulty with these soft-stemmed flowers, try inserting a thin stick or a stub wire up the fleshy stem. Don't attempt to arrange tulips in florist's foam as they continue to grow after they have been cut. After a few days you will find your tulips growing above all the other flowers and foliage.

The Arum lilies that have been included in the design are synonymous with Easter and capture the spirit of the festival. Traditionally, they decorate the church altar on Easter Sunday.

1 Take your tall glass vase and fill it with water. Cut a length of chicken wire to size and fold it into shape, so that it fills the vase easily but is not too massed so that you are unable to fit in the stems of your flowers. It should act in the same way as a rose bowl would. Now wrap the black velvet around the vase, bind it in place with the tasselled cord that has been chosen to match the amaranthus and let it trail down.

2 Place the amaranthus stems in the chicken wire, allowing the red flowers to hang down the outside of the vase to create the desired eerie and spooky effect.

3 Fill in with more stems of amaranthus and continue to build up the shape with smoke bush foliage or old man's beard, trimmed if necessary, to add some texture to the arrangement.

4 Finally, insert the dried Chinese lanterns into the vase to give the centrepiece the true Hallowe'en look, dotting them throughout the smoke bush foliage to add more autumnal colour throughout. Then place your prepared skull and candle on the trailing velvet, allowing enough room for the candle, when it is alight, to clear all the flowers and foliage in the vase.

1

2

3

4

MATERIALS
1 tall glass vase
Water
Chicken wire
1m (1 yd 3in) black velvet
About ½m (1½ft) silk cord with tassels
Scissors
5 stems of amaranthus, cut to size
1 bunch of smoke bush or old man's beard
1 bunch of dried Chinese lanterns
2 beeswax candles (one to drip wax on skull)
1 plastic skull (from a joke shop)
Floral fix

EASY LEVEL

A HALLOWE'EN CENTREPIECE

This special date marks a night that holds the perfect opportunity to throw a costume party. Choose a theme with supernatural flavour and give dress guidance on the invitation.

In this arrangement the candle was attached to the plastic skull with temporary floral fix that washes off under hot water. Wax was then dripped onto the skull from a lighted candle to create the sinister effect.

For the display itself a glass vase was wrapped in black velvet and bound with a red tasselled cord. The flowers were chosen for their eerie appearance and the dried Chinese lanterns for their resemblance to miniature pumpkins.

1 Cut two long lengths of chicken wire to form the cornucopia. Attach the two strips together side by side with the reel wire to make one wider strip. Roll this into a cone shape and then wrap in the hessian.

2 Once the cone shape is covered by the hessian, pin the fabric firmly into place. Then bind the hessian tightly with the natural raffia.

3 Take a short plank of wood, long enough to hold your cornucopia, and screw on it a length of thick, straight branch. This will then be used to hold the inner container in place.

4 Cut a slit in the hessian at the exact place that you require the support to pass through. Next cut a smaller piece of wood to a size that will fit inside the cone shape and sit on the end of the strong branch. This will act as a shelf for the inner container to sit on. Screw the shelf into position. Now secure the inner container to the shelf with the aid of floral fix. Hammer nails through the hessian and the chicken wire to hold the tail in place. Cut a small section of florist's foam to size and then wedge it into the bottom of the inner container to hold all the flowers in place. Top up the inner container with water.

1

2

3

INTERMEDIATE LEVEL

HARVEST FESTIVAL

This cornucopia is full of the rich, mellow colours of harvest time. It has been designed as a main table feature to highlight a Harvest Festival (or Thanksgiving) barn dance. Set the table until it is overflowing with the spoils of the harvest, or use the cornucopia design to enhance a buffet table on a similar occasion. The height of the *horn* itself will ensure the *plenty* it contains will be held well away from the food laid out on the table, leaving easy access for all the guests to get to the buffet.

Once the horn has been made it can be kept and re-used again and again for other similar celebrations. The design can also be altered so that it can be used for different themes. It could be easily changed into a Christmas decoration by using festive material and ribbons to bind around the cone shape and placing seasonal foliage among the flowers. You could also adapt the idea for a wedding celebration by using pastel silks as your covering and soft-coloured flowers.

5

6

MATERIALS
Chicken wire
Reel wire
Hessian sacking
Pins
Natural raffia
Short plank of wood
Thick, straight branch (from garden centres or florists)
Small piece of wood
1 screw
Screwdriver
Container
Floral fix
Hammer
Nails
Soaked florist's Wet foam (see p. 12)
1 bunch of hypericum, cut to size
1 bunch of wheat
1 bunch of dock, cut into short and long stems
1 bunch of thistles
1 bunch of Ambience roses, cut to size

7

8

5 Arrange the hypericum in the florist's foam. Position them carefully so that they create a free and natural style.

6 Next arrange the clumps of wheat in the container to give a country feel to the flowers and to fill out the shape of the harvest arrangement. Build up the foliage with the shorter stems of dock to support the large-stemmed flowers. Then randomly place the thistles throughout the foliage, keeping the stems quite long.

7 Next arrange the long stems of dock throughout the floral arrangement to give it some extra height and definition.

8 Finally, place the roses deep in the arrangement to give some extra colour and background depth to the completed cornucopia of flowers and foliage.

109

INDEX

ACKNOWLEDGMENTS

THE PUBLISHERS AND AUTHOR WOULD LIKE TO THANK THE FOLLOWING PEOPLE AND ORGANIZATIONS FOR THEIR GENEROUS HELP AND SUPPORT IN THE PRODUCTION OF THIS BOOK:

SUPPLIER OF ACCESSORIES AND PROPS

BARNUMS CARNIVAL NOVELTIES LTD
67 HAMMERSMITH ROAD, LONDON W14 8UY

THE DINING ROOM SHOP
68 WHITE HART LANE, BARNES, LONDON SW13 0PZ

FINAL TOUCH
10 BURNFOOT AVENUE, LONDON SW6 5EA

PETER PLACE
636 KINGS ROAD, LONDON SW3

THE STENCIL COMPANY LIMITED
20-21 HERONSGATE ROAD, CHORLEYWOOD, HERTS WD3 5BN
(Mail order for fabric paints 0923 285577/88)

THOMAS GOODE
19 SOUTH AUDLEY STREET, LONDON W1Y 5DN

TOBIAS AND THE ANGEL
64 WHITE HART LANE, LONDON SW13 0PZ

VARIATIONS AND THEMES
231 WESTBOURNE GROVE, LONDON W11 2SE

SPECIAL THANKS FROM THE AUTHOR TO

KIM CARTER AND PETER GRAYER FOR THEIR TIME AND ASSISTANCE.
CATE FOWLER AND ANDREW JONES FOR THEIR HELP IN THE PREPARATION OF THE MANUSCRIPT.
MARGOT AND ALAN DAVIS FOR LENDING SOME CROCKERY
SALLY PEARTON FOR HER TYPING OF THE MANUSCRIPT

AND SPECIAL THANKS TO

KATHIE GILL FOR PROOFREADING AND INDEXING

SANDRA AND PETER, BARBARA AND EDDIE, NICK AND CAROLINE, DAVID AND PAULINE AND JUDITH FOR THE USE OF THEIR HOMES FOR PHOTOGRAPHY. ROWHILL GRANGE, WILMINGTON, KENT DA2 7QH FOR THE USE OF THEIR HOTEL FOR THE PHOTOGRAPHY OF THE WEDDING AND CHRISTMAS SECTIONS *(see pp. 54, 67, 82–93)*

USEFUL ADDRESS

LONDON GRAPHIC CENTRE, 107/115 LONG ACRE, COVENT GARDEN, LONDON WC2E 9NT
(Paper and stationery suppliers)